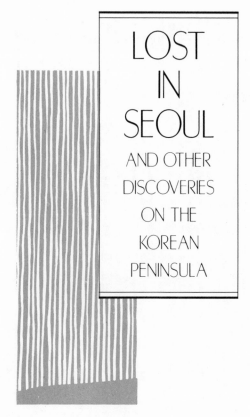

LOST
IN
SEOUL

AND OTHER
DISCOVERIES
ON THE
KOREAN
PENINSULA

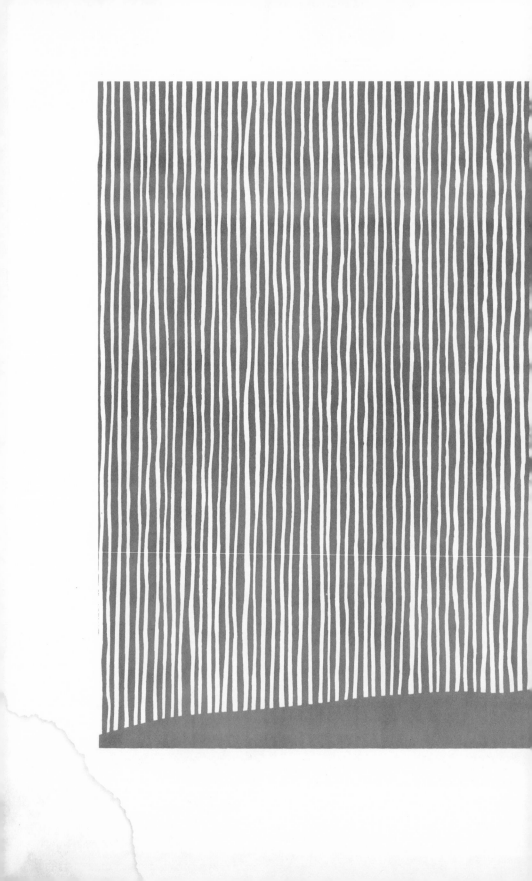

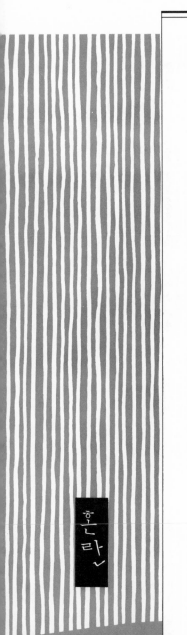

LOST IN SEOUL

AND OTHER DISCOVERIES ON THE KOREAN PENINSULA

MICHAEL STEPHENS

RANDOM HOUSE
NEW YORK

Library of Congress Cataloging-in-Publication Data

Stephens, Michael Gregory.
Lost in Seoul : and other discoveries on the Korean peninsula / by
Michael Stephens.
p.   cm.
ISBN 0-394-57482-6
1. Stephens, Michael Gregory—Journeys—Korea (South)   2. Authors,
American—20th century—Journeys—Korea (South)   3. Korea (South)—
Description and travel.   I. Title.
PS3569.T3855Z466   1990
818'.5403—dc20   [B]   89-42771

Manufactured in the United States of America
24689753
First Edition

Book design by JoAnne Metsch

For Okhee,
nae boo-in kwa chin-goo

That which moves is Heaven.
That which is still is Earth.
Associated with both
Motion and Stillness is Man.
—KING SEJONG

You can divide a thing in two, but its inseparability should be kept.
—YI HWANG

CONTENTS

AUTHOR'S NOTE

Because this is a work of creative nonfiction, and thus of imagination as much as of fact, I often play with chronology and detail for the purpose of creating a more authentic rhythm of experience—but never, I hope, at the risk of being dishonest to people or their landscape. I ask readers who are conversant with the subtleties of Korea's culture and recent past to make this leap of faith with me. The arc of the narrative starts in the 1970s and follows, roughly, a decade and a half, almost to the present. Nearly all the names, except those of public figures, have been changed; some of the characters are composites of several people I know in Korea. For my wife's family I have chosen the name Han as a generic Korean surname—the formal name for Korea is Dae Han Min Guk (Great Land of the Han People), and anyone familiar with Korea will know immediately that the Yi (pronounced Ee) court names were invariably

Yi or Min, not Han. Likewise, it is very rare indeed for successive generations in a family to have the same generational name (in this case, Hoon), as they do in the chapter "Tea at the Palaz of Hoon."

I wrote this book as the result of longstanding hospitality and kindness from many different people in Korea, making it almost impossible to express sufficient gratitude to all of them one by one. But I would be remiss not to thank Mr. and Mrs. Pyong-Yoo Minn, In-Hee Yoo, Sohn-Joo Minn (for help and advice with the Hangul design at the beginning of chapters), Mr. and Mrs. Chang-Kyong Kim, as well as various members of the "Han" clan. I also wish to thank Rob Wilson for his help and suggestions with the manuscript and Tim Rehwaldt for some typing. Finally, I am deeply indebted to my editor, Rebecca Saletan, for an abiding patience as I journeyed through various personal peaks and valleys writing this book, and for her careful editing of the manuscript; and I am likewise indebted to my agent Eric Ashworth, for his faith and encouragement of many years now. Lastly, I must thank Okhee, for her eyes and ears and family in Seoul.

Any errors are strictly the result of my own ineptitude and blind enthusiasm, not foremalice; any misreadings of Korean customs and manners are the result of similar impulses.

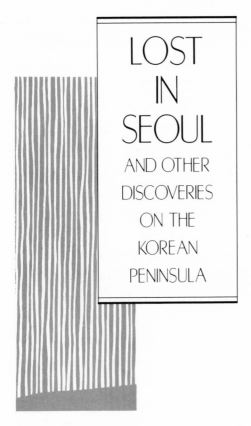

LOST
IN
SEOUL

AND OTHER

DISCOVERIES

ON THE

KOREAN

PENINSULA

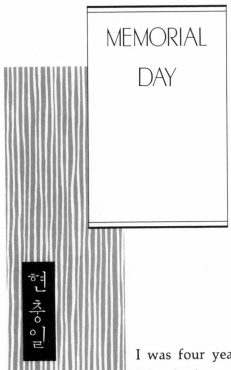

MEMORIAL
DAY

I was four years old when the Korean War broke out. My family lived in Brooklyn, but they were packing our belongings to move from a ghetto in East New York to the suburbs on Long Island. The United States and the Soviets had divided the Korean peninsula at the 38th Parallel after World War II, and while the North Korean soldiers broke over the DMZ and worked their way down Highway One into Seoul, I sat on the stoop of our house, looking at a box of metal soldiers in World War I helmets and uniforms. My next-door neighbor, a young sailor who had to report back to the Brooklyn Navy Yard to reboard his ship, had just given the toy soldiers to me; but within a matter of hours my two older brothers had taken the toy soldiers and made them their own through simple muscle and intimidation.

A week later one of my uncles pulled up in front of the old

brownstone at Marion and Rockaway and, after the movers left, heading east on Atlantic Avenue, everyone in the family piled into the cavernous Packard, bound for the Island. My uncle was a newspaperman, and on the drive out he and my father talked about the "police action" in Korea, though for the life of me, I had no idea what they meant. I pictured tin soldiers in World War I gear, slogging through mud and keeping America safe from our enemies.

But Korea surfaced daily in the new house, whenever I looked for the sports pages of the newspapers on the dining room table. The front pages were filled with photographs of the war (even then, the police action appeared to be a war). But it was not until the following Memorial Day that I had a firsthand glimpse of what the Korean War had done to people.

After the local parade, the village politicians assembled on the steps of town hall to make patriotic speeches, none of which I remember; but somewhere during the ceremony, various local heroes were introduced. Two World War I veterans were presented, rickety men in plaid jackets, balancing themselves on their canes like flamingos. Then came the onslaught of World War II vets, almost every father present; last and least the Korean War vets, a raggedy-assed contingent of young men with missing appendages, using canes, wheelchairs, and crutches to steady themselves. They were heroes, sort of, though nowhere near as esteemed as the World War II vets—but heroes nonetheless, and the crowd applauded them.

Afterward, my second oldest brother motioned for me to follow him, and together we headed for the playground at a nearby grammar school. As we walked, my brother bounced a Spaldeen on the pavement and carried a sawed-off broom handle on his shoulder, like a rifle. I thought we were going to play stickball, but instead of heading to the part of the school ground where we played ball, he trotted to the back of the Little League field and slipped through the fence and onto the property of Colonial Sand and Gravel—the sandpit.

"We're not supposed to be here," I said.

"Shuddup," my brother answered, and he sat down at the top of the hill overlooking the sandpit.

Down below, a bunch of kids were swimming in the muddy, typhoidal water of the sinkhole. Technically speaking, we had left our own town and were now in Cowtown, an imaginary place north of our home where all the delinquent boys seemed to live. I felt like Pinocchio in Candyland when I came here. The Island was not yet developed, and just beyond the sandpit were dairy farms and Bloody Hollow Woods. My mother had forbidden us to play here, but that didn't stop my brother.

Just then a commotion broke out in the waterhole, the boys diving and searching frantically in the water. It wasn't until the police and ambulance arrived that I understood what had happened. One of the boys had drowned. Later, a legend would grow up around that incident, the story being that the body was never recovered. I was always wary of the sandpit, but now I associated it with the darkest side of growing up, and the image of the unrecovered body resonated in my mind. I used to think that if the derricks in the adjacent quarry kept digging, eventually they would reach China, and if I imagined myself making that journey through the sandpit, invariably I wound up in Beijing—Peking in those days—upside down. Once in a while, I wound up in Korea.

My recurring sense of Korea surfaced in a dream that lasted for most of my childhood. I was standing in front of my family's old house on Marion Street in East New York, waiting to move to Long Island. The pea green, four-door Packard pulled up, and everyone got in and drove off—everyone, that is, but me. Somehow my family had forgotten that I was left behind, and there I stood, lonely and abandoned—orphaned. It was this feeling of being an orphan that most reminded me of Korea: every year the nuns at my school handed out yellow mitre boxes to fill with our pennies for the orphans left behind by the Korean War. Being an orphan meant everyone in your family getting into a Packard in Brooklyn and driving off to Long Island without you. That's what I thought it was like to be a child in Korea. If the derricks at the sandpit dug until they reached China, that was fine; but if they dug until they came to Korea, it was the loneliest feeling in the world.

When I was twelve, a few burnt-out caddies at the golf course where I worked were Korean War veterans, living from loop to loop, from one bottle of sweet wine to the next. They played poker in the caddy shack and went to Roosevelt and Belmont racetracks to play the ponies. They had Irish names like Meaney and Mooney, or nicknames like Daytona Don and Detroit; they were broken men in ways I couldn't yet fathom. One of these ghosts had survived the devastation at Chosun Reservoir, another had been a prisoner of war and had the hollowed-out eyes of a corpse.

In high school, I remember only the most oblique references to Korea. When my oldest brother enlisted in the Army, he speculated about whether he would be sent to Korea or Germany, and he wound up going to Germany. A next-door neighbor's older brother talked to us about Vietnam, the Central Highlands, the Montagnard tribesmen, Southeast Asia. He was a member of the first Green Beret A-team to go to South Vietnam. While still in my teens, I got to Europe the working-class way: my father worked on the Irish docks in Hell's Kitchen, and I was able to get seaman's papers and went to Northern Africa and Mediterranean Europe. I was taken with

two impressions that stayed with me through many voyages—
how *old* and *dirty* Europe was. It reminded me of something
George Orwell once said, that there was not an inch of the
continent that had not passed through someone's entrails. But
Asia was my goal, my idea of Manifest Destiny—not to con-
quer, but discover and appreciate the world west of continental
United States. Again, though, I didn't think of Korea, but
rather of Southeast Asia. I was about to sign on a resupply ship
for Danang when my union went on strike; I signed off the
boat and never returned.

It was not until I was an adult, living in New York City, and
heard friends talk about soulful Korean musicians, the Vietnam War winding down for America, that I became aware of
Korea. The most obvious sign of it, at the street level, was the
proliferation of Korean grocers. It was roughly around this
time that I met my wife, an opera singer, and a few weeks later
got married (a story for another volume). Since I never spoke
about Asia to anyone, knew little about opera, and was
thought never to consider marriage—I came from an odd family of ten children—everyone thought I was acting out on one
of my peculiar impulses. Five years later, still married, with a
two-year-old child, I found myself about to disembark from a
plane onto the tarmac of an airport on the outskirts of Seoul.

I step down from the ramp and take in the vertiginous world
at Kimpo Airport, the flatness of the foreground, granite
mountains skirting the perimeter in every direction. I try to
find one familiar detail to anchor myself, but there are none.
The Korean mountains—my wife says Vermont reminds her of
them—seem more like prototypes for the Chinese painting
genre known as Rivers and Mountains without End. Even the
sky is devoid of a familiar cerulean, instead it has the celadon

cast of a Koryo vase. The earthy faces of the workers on the tarmac are no help, nor are the stony countenances of the security guards near the arrivals building.

Even my sense of time has been dislocated. We'd left New York at seven Sunday evening—my wife Haeja and our daughter Fionna; but we'd crossed the Dateline and already it is Tuesday morning.

Haeja has come home for a reunion with her family after ten years' absence, half of which time she has been married to me, an American. She wants to see her mother, her siblings—especially her older sister Hae-Soon, who is her confidante—but particularly she has come to visit Grandma Oh, her late father's mother who raised her and is now very old. It's taken us so long to get here because of economics (no money), geography (too far away), and matters of state (my wife did not want to return until she'd become an American citizen).

Now that we've arrived, Haeja moves quickly into the terminal. I follow, holding Fionna's little hand while pulling along the baggage cart with our bags and trying to keep track of Haeja's green hat as it appears and disappears in the crowd. My wife is our umbilical cord to this new world, and I show my apprehension of losing her by squeezing my daughter's hand too tightly.

She has words enough already to let me know that I'm being too uptight. To her, Kimpo Airport might be Disneyland, the sights and sounds are so different from anything she's absorbed in her two years on this planet. But somewhere she has learned that Koreans love little children, and so has decided to accept as much love as they want to lavish on her; even before we have located Haeja's family, total strangers are approaching her to coo and bill, touch her cheek, whisper how pretty she is.

It seems like half of Seoul's population—a city more crowded than New York—has shown up to meet our flight.

"Yabo-saeyo!"

"An-yong-hasaeyo."

"Yabo! Iri wha!"

The voices resonate and overlap like a fugue, shouting *hello—hey, there—husband, come on!* The men sound like echoes from the earth, but the women speak *Hangul-mal,* Korean, as if it were a Romance language, the vowels light, airy, and open, their pitch exquisite.

An old woman pushes through the airport crowd, selling peeled, sliced apples. The smell of hot noodles scents the air. All around us ceremonial greetings are made by knots of relationships, homebodies embracing the returned travelers. Carts filled with luggage knock past our knees.

Finding the Hans seems like an impossible proposition, but within seconds one of the family's assistants races over and relieves me of our baggage, escorting us through the crowd to an island of relations at the rear of the terminal. Instantly Haeja is in her mother's arms, then in her older sister's arms, then hugging and kissing her brothers and sisters, her nieces and nephews. She cries like a baby.

Now Fionna is clutching my hand tightly, unsure who all these people are, picking her up, passing her around, kissing her, pinching her cheeks. With a kick here, a push there, she manages to free herself and run back into my arms, from where she gives everyone a serious frowning appraisal, not relinquishing her scowl until her mother tells her that these are her Korean family.

"Well," Fionna says, huffy but willing to reconcile. "Okay." Everyone breaks into laughter, then applause, even bystanders.

"Aye, *yae-pu-da,*" Mrs. Han shouts, "Ah, so pretty." Meanwhile, brothers and sisters come forward to me, either to shake hands or, western style, to give and receive a kiss.

To the side stands Haeja's older sister, Hae-Soon, with her husband, Mr. Lee, a great big man with a broad smile and a strong handshake, who wears a dark business suit, white shirt, and tie. Mr. Lee is an engineer. Hae-Soon, like the other women of the family, wears a fashionably conservative dress, her hairdo and makeup very understated, very subtle. Next to them stand their three children, two very pretty girls and a five-year-old boy, Chul-Hee, who appears overcome by the sight of his aunt, his American uncle, and his new Korean-American cousin.

"You must be my nephew," I say to him, and he wraps himself inside the folds of his mother's dress and begins to cry. Mr. Lee laughs and tells him not to worry, I am only an uncle, not a ghost.

"You must get your hair cut," Mrs. Han tells her immigrant daughter. Haeja's hair is frizzed into a wild, Medusalike theatricality, reaching far down her back. Her mother wears a dark business suit and a hairdo that seems to have been inspired by Jacqueline Onassis.

Mrs. Han adds, "And you wear too much makeup."

Haeja wears a very flamboyant eye shadow of her own invention, which I find quite exotic and beautiful.

Mrs. Han takes me by the arm, as we head for the parking lot, and assays my getup skeptically. Taking in the rumpled olive green linen suit I'd bought the week before in New Haven, she adds, "Michael needs a new suit."

The lead car pulls up, an old black Mercedes sedan; Haeja, Fionna, and I climb in back, Mr. and Mrs. Han in front. Several other Korean-made cars, carrying the rest of the family, follow us out of the airport.

"He needs a new suit," Mrs. Han repeats to Haeja.

"He doesn't wear suits," Haeja answers, in a fog of jet lag and homecoming blues.

"What is all this hair on your head?" Mrs. Han asks, "and all these curls down your back. You're a mother now."

"It's the style," moans Haeja.

"Where?" her mother asks.

"I'm tired," answers my wife.

I can see that Haeja now has some new roles in her life since stepping onto the tarmac at Kimpo. She is a wife and mother, two important roles to add to her repertoire in this familial world, where she is already daughter, sister, and aunt, each with its own complex decorum. In America, Haeja was able to assume these roles with little effort; but in Seoul, she must change hats, not just socially, but even in terms of the syntax of her native tongue—each of these grammatical changes is more deferential than the last.

"Yom-chae," Mr. Han laughs, ruffling Fionna's hair. A *yom-chae* is a spoiled child, but in a precious kind of way—a little genius, if you will.

On the road east along the Han River into Seoul, rice paddy gives way to storefronts, low-rise apartment complexes, and factories. The tall, narrow poplars and drooping willows along the roadside are replaced by people and cars, trucks and buses—and more people. Only the yellow-brown granite mountains, forever in a haze in the background, continue even into the city, their jagged peaks everywhere on the horizon.

In order to settle the turbulence that lingers in my stomach from the flight and regain equilibrium in my inner ear, I focus on particular people and things in the landscape, locking my eyes on them. An old woman in a print blouse and baggy pants like bloomers, her face pinked by sunlight and frost, hefts a huge bundle, and pads off with the precarious load on top of her head. Old men in jade silk jackets and baggy silver pants smoke long pipes and talk with each other on a street corner, while all around the commerce and industry of the city race past them. Others, their bodies frail as scarecrows, carry hemp A-frames on their backs. Younger men ride by on bicycles, hauling impossibly gigantic loads of pots and pans, soda bottles, and soup dishes.

Girls in blue jumpers and white blouses walk in groups of four. Boys in brown-and-white speckled camouflage utility fatigues strut, shoulder to shoulder, in the opposite direction. In their midst are men in dark business suits, women in fashionable clothing, the hems of their dresses nearly to their ankles, and little children playing ball. Green and white buses belch out diesel fumes from highbodied frames, flatbed trucks weave through the net of the thick traffic, functional black jeeps swerve back and forth drunkenly in the lanes, through a soup of Korean, Japanese, and American cars, all of them painted a lustrous, austere black.

It is another busy morning in Seoul, a city whose inhabitants work seven days a week and never take vacations, a city without boundaries, sprawling out of its bowl-like valley with a perpetual gray blue mist of pollution sitting over it, reaching its fingers up the mountainsides and over them, fanning out in every compass direction, including that mysterious fifth one, the center, where horizons disappeared long ago, and things now strive toward a vertical nature.

About every third building, there is an excavation, a concrete foundation with bamboo and rope scaffolding going up, burnished men and women lugging bushels of bricks onto the site as other men work antlike, laying bricks and mortar in a row. The music is jackhammers, honking horns, whistles, shouts, and combustion; its rhythm is frenetic, double-time, an uptempo blues.

Every once in a while, the incredible drabness of the concrete streets and the brickface and stucco façades is punctuated by the flutter of irridescent colors emanating from a *hanbok,* the traditional dress: a billowy, long sleeve with rainbow stripes catches the eye.

"So this is Seoul," Mr. Han says, gesturing with a sweep of his hand across the windshield. The driver focuses all his energy on the task of maneuvering the car. Haeja's mother has shifted in the passenger seat, the better to see us.

"What do you think?" she asks me.

"It's, it's beautiful," I say, "it's very nice. It's, it's so different from what I imagined." Jet travel has turned me into an inarticulate mass of protoplasm in a wrinkled linen suit, my eyes bulging out of my head, my senses overwhelmed. My dreams of Korea had been of Genghis and Kublai Khan, Mongol invaders and Siberian horsemen, the Altaic tribes, the primitive witchcraft of the folk-healers, the fortune-tellers of whom Haeja has told me so much, the palmists, the face-readers, the diviners. Rarely, if ever, did I think of Seoul as what it is, a huge megalopolis like New York or Los Angeles, its gears oiled for industry, its wheels pumping out leather coats, shoes, fan blades, plastics, and metals.

"Too crowded," says Mrs. Han. "Too many cars. And too noisy today."

Mr. Han smokes and says nothing, staring at the traffic ahead.

"A few minutes more," he says, "and we'll be home."

I'm still disoriented from the trip, my ears clogged and unaccustomed to sea level, mouth cottony, and head dried out, so I let Haeja pick up the slack in the conversation. Fionna looks out the back window of the car, waving to her cousins behind us.

My mind drifts to legends of famous women entertainers known as *kisaeng,* who danced and sang and seduced with their songs and poems throughout the various dynasties. I think of Hwang Jini, the greatest woman poet of Korea, and the patriot Nongae who seduced a Japanese general in the sixteenth century, only to lead him to a precipice, where she pushed him over and lept to her death. Hongnang writes:

> *Buds open in night rain*
> *Remember me*

Suddenly, an air-raid siren explodes across the landscape and the car comes to an abrupt halt; all around us the traffic has stopped and people are getting out of their cars.

Haeja, Fionna, and I climb out after the Hans. The siren whines and whines incessantly, and I half expect that we'll all be diving for cover under the cars, hands over our heads, waiting for incoming artillery from the lunatic communist horde in the North; I imagine South Korean soldiers appearing at one end of this boulevard and North Korean troops at the other, with us civilians caught in the crossfire—those lucky enough to find a safe doorway will live to talk about this latest escalation of hostilities. I'm already composing the copy to be smuggled out of the city at dusk via medivac helicopter to an American military base in Japan, where it'll be wired to *The New York Times*—which will of course run it on the front page under my byline.

Cars around me continue to idle or have gone dead. Up and down the wide boulevard, people cluster together silently, their heads bowed, as if in prayer. The interminable hum of commerce, production, progress is dead, and a hush descends on the center of the city, now as still as the most remote rice paddy.

My fear dissipates into a growing curiosity, but it seems inappropriate to ask questions, so I try without success to read the expressions on the faces of the pedestrians. Wait it out, I think. This can't go on forever.

Across the street a movie poster in lurid Day-Glo colors advertises *Star Wars.* The window next to the theater is stacked with plastic blades for electric fans. In front of another shop giant earth-colored urns are stacked. A worker stands beside his bicycle; behind the seat, cartons of soda are piled ten feet high. Up the block, young soldiers stand rigidly at attention, their weapons at their sides.

Over the tile roofs of the low buildings, I see thousands of tiny houses salted into the hillside. At the top of one mountain, a huge neon cross proclaims JESUS SAVES! In another direction, I see a Buddhist temple, and my eyes freeze on a swastika painted just under the rooftop—I know that a thousand years before the Nazis this was a symbol of love and spiritual nurturing.

The overall mood is one of solemnity, as if we are participants at some outdoor revival meeting and the preacher has paused before beginning a prayer. I try to partake of this feeling, but I can't figure out my own part in the drama. Whatever ritual is taking place, though, isn't about to stop because I'm alienated by it.

Over the course of a few minutes, the air-raid sirens don't exactly die out, but they slowly fade into a lingering buzz in my ears. At some point that I can't discern in the ceremony, people here and there begin to lift their heads slowly: first a change in expression, then a shoulder twitch, arms and legs move, and some walk back to their cars, get in and drive off. Others linger on, embracing the stillness and silence. Pedestrians frozen in midstride at the outset of the sound thaw themselves out and stride away down the sidewalk. The city sounds return.

"What happened?" I ask as we get into the car.

"It's all right," says Mrs. Han. Her mood has changed to one of subdued introspection.

"It is Memorial Day," Mr. Han says finally, caught up as well in the collective quiet.

I think of the millions with heads bowed moments earlier, each of their lives touched in some way by the war. Was there even one who hadn't lost a relative to it? I knew that marrying Haeja meant eventually dealing with her family, but what *that* meant I couldn't know—what "Korea" is as a collective entity, what it means to its citizens. I feel as if I've stumbled gracelessly into a private moment in a nation's life, with my foreigner's eyes and my incorrigible need to know. The Hans had become one with their nation as it mourned its dead, and I was both impressed and chilled.

A calm settles over me, more exhaustion than spiritual release, as we near the skyscrapers of downtown Seoul. In my vast ignorance about this world I am entering, I quickly feel right at home. Filial piety, virtue, proper conduct, righteousness—I have only a vague notion of the spiritual foundations of this new world. I wonder how useful in this orbit are my knowledge of basketball, open-form American poetry, western drama, Buster Keaton, "I Love Lucy," and Thelonious Monk.

Because I have married a Korean woman, I realize now that I also married into a Korean family and, by extension, I am now

16

part of the Korean world, a citizen of the realm. Now I have come home, I have arrived—albeit upside down, topsy-turvy, even backward. I am curious about what life will be like in this family, living and breathing among them, I sense an opening there. Will there be other moments of calm so deceptively concussive, other tensions so seemingly peaceful? I find myself contemplating again the childhood riddle of the sandpit, wondering if my first impressions were not the most apt after all. Only now does it occur to me that the sirens sounded, not because of invasion, but because of memory.

As Haeja speaks Korean with her parents, I picture Jack London riding into Pyongyang—on a Korean pony no bigger than a Newfoundland dog, he said, the year 1904. All about him a war between Japan and Russia raged on the peninsula, and he wrote of "apathetic Koreans too lazy to get out of the way." He was a big galoot, an American yahoo, and it never occurred to him that the outsiders like himself were unbalancing the sovereignty of a nation. Instead he wrote, in a dispatch to the San Francisco *Examiner,* of how he "suffered at the hands of inhospitable and insulting Koreans." Henri Michaux had a better take on these people: he called them the blues singers of Asia.

Then I fall, not into a pattern of English thoughts, but into another kind of silence, one that is an adjunct to that greater sound which had enveloped the city. When I come out of it, we have arrived at the Hans' doorstep, a beautifully restored summer palace north of Kyung-Bok Palace and right next door to Chung Hwa Dae, the Blue House, the presidential mansion.

There is an explosion of noise, as household assistants run from the back gate, yattering away, arguing over who is to carry what suitcases.

17

An-yong-ha-sae-yo, they say, bowing. Hello, they say, literally, are you at peace? Peace be with you. Again and again, deeper and deeper, the maids and housemen, the workers, the assistants, bow and bow, saying, *"An-yong-ha-sae-yo, an-yong-ha-sae-yo."*

LOST
IN
SEOUL

The air is thick with heat and humidity in the maze of alleyways in Namdaemun Market. Monsoon rains are only moments away. Already I have changed my sweat-soaked clothing twice, and it is only a little after noon. It reminds me of the beginning of Robert Stone's *Dog Soldiers:* a man named Converse sits on a bench in the shade facing Tu Do Street in Saigon and says to an American woman sitting nearby, "Well, we'll have some weather pretty soon." In a previous life I might have found the climate here heavy with foreboding, like Conrad's jungle heat. In Seoul, I can only think of it as weather, soupy and uncomfortably visible, and we are going to have some of it shortly. In Los Angeles, a day like this might provoke an air-quality alert; air pollution in Seoul is an emblem of pride, it means that the factories are running full tilt and the economy's booming. Any day this nation will slough off that label "third world": every country has weather, but only industrial powers have pollution.

South Gate Market is equally thick with people out shopping for bargains in the stalls and tiny shops that line the winding lanes. Every once in a while a black sedan inches through the crowd, and I step inside a doorway so my toes don't get run over.

Young girls sit behind tiny counters in the underground bazaars. Many of them rest their heads on their arms, which are laid across the counters like goods, and some are sound asleep. It is a little past one o'clock, and already most of the women have been up for eleven hours. Some of them, after finishing work at the market, may go to a second job as hostess in a drinking house, get home around ten or eleven, sleep for a few hours, and then return to the stalls in time for the early wholesalers and shopowners. Customers shout, push and shove. A few bull through Haeja and her sister, Hae-Soon, as if they were not there at all. Unventilated, the basements reek of fermented vegetables and sweat and the artificial odor of new clothing. The temperature is at least twenty degrees warmer than the torrid outside. We negotiate around bodies, stepping sideways, inhaling, moving on. When we stop to look at fabrics or clothing, always there are several people behind us, pushing into our backs, either waiting to look at the same merchandise or anxious to press on to other stalls.

With each day that passes the utilitarian, western-style, drab business suits and unimaginative conservative dresses of Seoul give way a little to more fashionable dress. With a good eye and some patience, Haeja and Hae-Soon will be able to find clothing for a fraction of the price they might pay at one of the big department stores like Shinsegae or Midopa, which are, in turn, much cheaper than American department stores—not to mention the ones in Tokyo. Very often South Gate Market is stocked with overruns of merchandise going to more expensive stores. Other times, the things are imitations, bootlegs or knockoffs, and some of them are very good. I hate shopping, and our progress in these basements is a snail's pace, yet I am entertained by the theatrics of the market stalls, the bartering, haggling, shouting and screaming, the tight press of people everywhere.

A paunchy, balding American soldier behind us, with his own family in tow, accidentally bumps into me and apologizes.

"Forget about a decent interval in Namdaemun," he says. "Down here you move as slow as if you're searching for land mines on a jungle trail."

"There you go," I say, noticing that with the infrequency of spoken English in my life, already I have reverted to the jargon of the American soldiers that I occasionally overhear in the street.

Haeja and Hae-Soon, unlike their mother and younger sisters, are not infected with "shopping fever," this frenzy to buy and buy, as though the money or the merchandise were about to disappear any second. They have discussed in advance what they are looking for, and they only stop at a stall when it seems to offer what they want. Since there is no place in the basements to try on clothing, one sister holds a dress up to the other.

"*Un-nee,* how does it look?"

"It is *you,* sister." Haeja buys it.

At the next stall, Haeja holds up a dress and asks my opinion.

"Nice," I say noncommittally.

"He always says that," she tells her sister, who smiles and flows onward into the crowd as gracefully as a dancer.

An *ajima* pushes through the crowd, hawking her tray of cut apples. They look delicious, fresh and juicy, and vendors rouse themselves to buy a slice or two.

"How much longer?" I ask.

"Be patient," I'm told.

"Maybe I'll wander around by myself and meet you later."

"No!" Haeja screams, and several people turn to look.

I am reminded of the pervasive fear of loss that haunts this city from the war. Things have a way of disappearing; people walk out the door and never come back.

Men, especially.

It happened to those close to Haeja, Hae-Soon, their mother, their aunts, their cousins, their classmates, their friends. Probably everyone in this market could name someone who has disappeared.

I grew up with bitter old men cursing the Korean peninsula because they fought a dirty war here. Their minds were filled with images of rubble, gutted landscapes, biting chill, Chinese hordes, napalm, claymore mines, frozen ghosts. The mountains had numbers instead of names, and some rises were so stripped of greenery that even to call them hills was somehow to miss the point. In the afternoon my neighborhood bar on upper Broadway is filled with men who came of age and lost their dreams in Korea a few years before Elvis Presley recorded his first song. Some lost arms and legs; some lost buddies. Others lost their spirits and find solace now in the dark of afternoon bars, recounting war stories to others who share their bitterness. Still others trained the next generation for war, becoming lifers in the military. But most of them carry Korea around with them like a dark secret, and speak about it only when asked; and even then their responses tend to be perfunctory, embarrassed even. Korea was no World War II, it had none of that glory, and yet, for my own generation it also had nothing of the aftershock, none of the divisiveness of Vietnam. More than fifty thousand Americans died in three bloody years at the beginning of the 1950s, and still no monument to their heroism has been erected in Washington. Like their dreams, the paperwork got lost, not in a combat zone but in a government bureaucracy.

We wander deeper into the labyrinth of alleyways in the market. I stop to watch and listen to a legless man bouncing along on his buttocks and pushing with his muscular arms a low cart filled with handkerchiefs and socks. He has a portable microphone with a loudspeaker, and he croons romantic pop songs to passersby. People drop coins into his cup and take socks or handkerchiefs in return. He is a good-looking man, and his voice is richly textured, almost professional. I drop a thousand won note (a dollar and change) into his cup and take a pair of socks.

"Thank you," he says in English, which startles me. I want to ask him how he lost his legs. His arms are strong looking, his chest broad, his neck muscles taut.

"Where did you learn to sing so well?" I ask.

"In my mother's womb," he answers.

"And your English," I ask, "where did you learn it?"

"I was a ROK Tiger," he says. "Vietnam."

When I look up, I no longer see Haeja and Hae-Soon.

"My wife," I say, "I think I lost her. I'd better go. Good luck." As I walk off down the narrow, serpentine lane, I hear him singing a song by Cho Yong-Pil, Korea's pop hero; it's on the radio everywhere these days. But Haeja and Hae-Soon are not in any of the shops, and when I retrace my steps, the singer has vanished as well. A street vendor holds a melon before my face and asks if I want to buy, another holds out a pair of bootleg Levi's, an old woman rattles a Bee-Gees tape: "Bargain," she says, "discount prices for GIs."

After a half hour of walking up and down the narrow lanes, being pushed and shoved, squeezing past crowds of shoppers, I remember that the sisters were going to meet their mother at the Hyatt hotel, which I think is in Itae-Won. I hail a Pony cab outside the Market.

"Plenty of good times in Itae-Won," the driver says.

He drops me off in front of Victory Market, where a lot of young Koreans and Americans from the nearby Eighth Army Headquarters are rummaging through the clothing stalls. Curbside carts sell everything from fake Rolex watches to Polo clothing and Calvin Klein jeans. The English used by the hawkers and vendors is chopped and splayed, nearly unrecognizable, even if the merchandise is familiar. One of these hawkers holds up a Louis Vuitton bag and says, "On sale today only, Ruby Tone bags." I think of the caricature of East Asia that has resulted from American occupations, of how *r*'s and *l*'s mistakenly get used, but Ruby Tone is downright musical, like the title of an old bebop tune.

The lure of Itae-Won is the foreigners, mostly Americans, who flock here. The U.S. Eighth Army Headquarters is across the street, and soldiers ply the streets, looking for a good time on R and R. Those who are married search for bargains with their wives and children at the stands on the street, the stalls in the crowded alleys winding up the hills here, and in the bargain basements in every building. The specialties of Itae-Won include eelskin coats, wallets, and belts; leather goods of all sorts; surplus or rip-off American designer clothing, T-shirts, tube socks, underwear (in American sizes), shoes, sneakers; and inexpensive tailor-made suits and overcoats.

Koreans fill the alleyways, but none of them is shopping. The locals go to East Gate or South Gate for bargains. Here, they sell to Americans, which recalls black market days after the war when Koreans came to buy Spam, turkeys, ice cream, peanut butter, Welch's jelly, Ritz crackers, and American greenbacks.

The Korean sense of what is trendy is uncanny. Where once hot Levi's filled the stalls, now Polo sportswear is draped. The tailor-made suit shops are giving way to leather goods and athletic equipment. The only constant in Itae-Won from the war years is prostitution, which hardly exists in the daylight hours but after dusk turns Itae-Won into a red-light district. The women who work the streets range from scabby and downtrodden hookers to beautiful, college-educated painted ladies who cater to generals and business executives. The bars are less Korean in style, too, and are lit like American road-houses, red and satiny blue the dominant colors, with juke-boxes screeching out the latest hard-driving rock 'n' roll.

Finally I make my way up the steep hill to the hotel, which overlooks Itae-Won and the southern part of Seoul, the Han River, and the new buildings going up south of the river.

I sit in the lobby on a big, comfortable sofa and order a coffee, taking in the magnificent view. Across from me several American and Korean soldiers are trying to drink themselves into oblivion, ordering glass after glass of Johnny Walker Black, beer, and appetizers to settle their stomachs. A couple of them, my age, are talking about their days in Vietnam, while the older ones reminisce about the Korean War. The Koreans among them speak passable English, and the American cadences sound almost like poetry to me, especially the musical speech of the American South.

When the waiter comes over, one of the younger Americans points to a red-faced Korean, "Give the gook another drink."

"I am *not* a gook," the Korean says, indignantly. "Hey, Billy, have you ever seen me skin a snake alive with my teeth?"

"I seen him, Billy," a red-haired redneck says. "Don't get Sergeant Kwang started."

The Korean sergeant laughs and beats his chest. "I am not a gook, I'm supergook!" It brings down the house. They laugh, cough, spew, spit up whiskey, patting and swatting each other, almost rolling on the floor. Sergeant Kwang makes a toast to his American friends.

But I still don't see anything of the sisters or their mother, and I'm beginning to worry. I decide that maybe I should go back to Samchung-dong. I go outside, hail a Pony cab, and tell the driver I want to go to Samchung-dong, Chongro-ku, near Kyung-Bok Palace, I say. The driver nods, revs his engine, and peels out, sending me flying backward into my seat as he winds out of the hotel area and along the mountain roads at this southern extremity of Nam San, the great mountain in the center of the city.

"A nice evening," he says.

"Thank you, I am fine," I answer.

"Businessman?" he asks.

"I'm from New York," I tell him.

"Ah," he says, "out for a good time."

"The weather has been good," I say.

"Good, good," he answers, "then I'll show you a good time."

North or south, in this darkness, who knows. I can't tell, that's for sure, so I sit back, leaving the directions to the driver. As he drives he talks to me in English and in Korean and sometimes in a pidgin of English and Korean, about the New York Yankees, the Los Angeles Dodgers. He tells me there are some good baseball teams in Korea, he talks about some boxers I never heard of, how the low-weight divisions are dominated by Koreans, WBA, WBC, the alphabet of boxing. His son is a baseball player, he tells me, not a boxer; his wife wants them to emigrate to America so that the boy can attend a good college, some place in Arizona or Florida with a baseball program, he says, nothing fancy but a good team, that's what he wants for his son. But first his son must go into the Army for a few years. He says, his uncle in the country speaks of a fairly good rice planting this spring, all the signs are there for a good season. Backbreaking work, he says, he did it as a boy, but then after his military duty, he came to the big city like all the other farm boys. He is from Cholla Province, he says—do I know Cholla Province? The revolutionaries, I say. *No, no, no, no,* he says—Cholla is the province of poets, of great singers, of artists, and thinkers. Other people, especially those big shots from Kyong-Sang Pukdo, say that Cholla breeds revolution, but it is not true. Cholla is the land of invention, he tells me, where Benjamin Franklin would have come from, where Thomas Edison would have come from, where that man who invented the computer would have come from, if they had been Korean.

"If they had been Korean," he repeats.

He tells me that he lives in such-and-such neighborhood on the outskirts of Seoul that I've never heard of. He has a little garden there, where he grows cabbage, peppers, and corn, he even has a pear tree.

"You can't stop being a farmer," he says, "just because you move to the city and drive a taxi."

He turns around frequently as he speaks and I ask him to pay

27

attention to the road. In this gloaming light all I can see is his one gold front tooth, reflecting the light from the cars behind us. His face is a blotchy red, what, as children, we used to call Irish skin, pale and easily tarnished by the elements. Perhaps it is from drinking too much *maggoli,* rice wine, or *soju,* grain alcohol. He does not drive like a sober man.

From farming, he moves to entertainment, cataloguing his favorite actors. Burt Reynolds, he says, better than Marlon Brando, and he enjoys watching American Army network news and other shows, to practice his English, and also to keep up on events important to Americans that aren't always covered in the local news. He says that he has been watching *The Rockford Files* lately, and that James Garner is a really fine actor, and a good man, too.

The cab goes over the Third Han River Bridge into New Seoul.

"You need comfort," the driver says in English.

"Just get me home," I say.

"Relax," he tells me.

The riverbed is dry, and looks more like a ravine than a river. A fishing scow sits dry-docked in the middle of it. Pools of water reflect the city lights. I have heard that when the monsoons arrive, the river sometimes rushes over the edge of the bridges, and they have to be closed, but it's hard to imagine that dry patch that separates the two Seouls ever flowing or churning.

I realize too late that we are going south instead of north. *"Stop!"* I shout.

"It's all right," he says.

"Chongro-ku!" I shout, pointing to the north, behind me.

"No problem," he says, lights a cigarette and offers me one. He drives past the new apartment complexes on the banks of the river. Here the side streets are crowded with love hotels, slinky barbershops, "stand bars" (a Korean version of American saloons), massage parlors, sashimi houses, drinking houses.

Wasn't I told not to go out by myself?

"Relax," the driver repeats, puffing on his cigarette. He whistles off-key, weaving in and out of the traffic of other taxis and black sedans and medium-sized trucks and the blue and green oversized Saehan buses belching out exhaust fumes.

"Businessman?" he asks.

"Yeah, yeah, sure," I say, "now turn around and drive north."

His skinny arms grip the wheel tightly as though someone were going to take away his taxi at any moment. At a stoplight, his lights turned off, he turns and leers at me. "Show you good time down here," he says.

"Turn around, mister," I say, trying to sound like a drill sergeant. "Or I'm going to get out here."

"Here?" he asks, pulling over to the curb, and then tallies up the fare on his meter. I gesture a U-turn with my hands, pointing behind me—north, north.

"Thank you, thank you," he says.

I pay and get out of the cab. The night is already going from cool to chilly and the hum is back in the air. I pick a street at random, then turn up another and wind around a bend and go through a series of alleys, until finally I find one of those oversized orange telephones.

"Where are you?"

"I'm in the south."

"Where?"

"Let's see"—I look around—"I just walked off Teheran Street."

"Where?"

"Like in Iran," I say. "Teheran."

"I never heard of it."

"It's one of those new streets in New Seoul, you know," I say. "I'm south of the Han River."

"South of the Han River? What are you going there?"

"I got lost—I mean the taxi took me in the wrong direction," I say.

A bunch of children stand around me—girls in dirty cotton blouses and boys in T-shirts and dungarees or jogging pants with canvas sneakers, the backs of their shoes pressed down like slippers—all of them staring quietly until one of the little girls decides to giggle, which ignites all of them to giggle, and I can hardly hear myself talk.

"Who's there?"

"I'm alone," I say, "but I'm calling from a telephone on the street, and a bunch of street kids are standing around listening to me talk on the telephone."

"Take a taxi," I'm told.

"Okay," I say, "don't worry."

The telephone goes dead, and when I deposit another coin to call back, I can't get a dial tone. I walk north and come on a restaurant called Number One Sashimi. I go inside. I look around. Empty. Two surprised waitresses come forward. They probably don't have many American customers. The chef behind the sushi bar bows, but he also looks surprised.

"Table for one?" a waitress asks.

"I'm looking for someone," I say.

"Raw fish?" one waitress asks. "Sure, we gots lotta raw fish."

I try sign language, body language, a little English; I gesture, I grunt, what's the use, they don't understand, and I don't understand either. I ask for a beer, which the waitress brings.

30

I pay and sip it, rubbing my back. The other girl comes over, rubs her own back, makes a sympathetic face. "Next door," she points, rubbing her back. Curious, I get up and go outside. I see a spinning red, white, and blue barber pole, so I go up the narrow, slanted stairway and enter a small parlor where two women in royal blue uniforms are manicuring their nails and a tough-looking balding little man, wearing a white barber's smock, is reading a sports magazine.

"Massaji," the girl closer to me says, laughing.

They giggle like the little girls outside by the telephone, and I think I could make a million dollars on Korean television the way I make women giggle in this town.

One of the girls takes me down the hall, and the tough-looking barber follows.

They sit me in a barber chair and wrap a bib around me; he wets my hair and starts to cut it with his scissors, and I say aloud, "I can't believe this is happening."

"Trim," he says, then goes ahead with his cutting without the least bit of interest in my response.

"Apples," I say in Korean, and he nods as if addressing his idiot brother's idiot son.

Another girl, smiling, comes into the cubicle and removes my shoes and socks; she washes my feet like she was Mary Magdalene, dries them, cuts my toenails, scrapes away brittle skin from the callouses. When the barber finishes, the first girl gives me a shampoo, still giggling, then says again, "Massaji." What the hell, I say, and she pulls on my legs and pulls on my arms, using the chair for leverage. She pushes one of her legs into the chair as she pulls on my arm, flips me on my side and lets her fingers ripple along my back muscles, which begin to contract, ah, that gets my attention. She jiggles her wrist back

31

and forth, like a crapshooter with a fistful of dice. "You want," she says, jiggling her wrist, and then, "okay," she says, and she is about to unzip my fly and massage me good.

A soldier comes into the cubicle and the woman stops dead. His jaw is rocklike, his cheeks are made of granite, his complexion is yellow-brown like the mountains. He is wearing utility camouflage, and the safety is off his automatic weapon, a plastic fantastic, the M16. He is young, but his jutty martial gestures make him seem older. He means business, I can see, and he asks me who I am and what I am doing here and please sir give your name and what is your country of origin.

The girl raises the barber chair to a sitting position and stands next to me with her hands on my shoulders.

"What is the matter?" she asks the soldier, but he does not answer, he is waiting for my response.

"I live in the north," I say.

He looks puzzled.

"Chongroku," I say, giving him the address and telephone number. "I am visiting," I say, "I am a . . ." and "I'll be leaving in a few months, just visiting family, taking in the sights. . . ."

"The sights?" he asks.

"Yes," I say, "Seoul is a very beautiful place."

He grunts.

I tell him that a taxi driver took me in the wrong direction, I was having a drink at the Hyatt, I was supposed to meet my wife and her sister there, but I lost them back at Namdaemun Market, wandered over to Itae-Won, then up to the hotel, got in the cab, the driver took me in the wrong direction, and here I am. I got lost, I tell him, I didn't want a haircut, no massage, certainly not what this girl is proposing. But I can see that the soldier is singularly uninterested in my account.

"You are aware that there is an air raid?" he asks.

"No, I was not."

"Did you hear the sirens?"

I did not.

He grunts again: "Your name, sir?"

I tell him.

"Employer?"

Visiting family, I say.

"Employer?" he asks again.

"Self," I say.

"Self?"

He asks me again who my employer is, and this time I do not answer. His eyes are dark and edgy. "Stay here," he says, and goes out.

The girl lathers my face, makes the chair horizontal again, and takes out a straight razor, which she hones on a leather strap attached to the chair. She hums what sounds like Vivaldi. I suddenly remember a friend telling me about Vietcong barbers who cut your hair in the daytime, your throat at night. I think about the mafioso, Albert Anastasia, gunned down in a barbershop in New York.

"No shave," I say.

"Okay," she says, and proceeds to shave me.

"American soldier?" she asks.

"No, no," I say, "I'm visiting."

"Oh, businessman," she says.

"What the hell," I say, and she smiles, as though I just told her she had a gorgeous face. But her face is tough and worn, even though she doesn't appear to be that old.

She places a hot towel over my face, and the steam feels good. She massages my arms and legs again, my chest and belly, and as she is about to unzip me, again I hear the soldier's combat boots thudding up the narrow stairway, through the outer room, and into the cubicle, where the hot towel still covers my face.

"Name," the soldier says.

I tell him.

"Nationality," he says, and I tell him that.

"Passport," he says.

"Left it back where I live," I say.

"Occupation," he says, and again I tell him, and again he glares at me. Then I see him almost smile, before he quickly recaptures the glare and shrugs his shoulders at the girl as if to say, What are we to do with people like him? He punches me gently in the arm and gestures for me to follow him. I walk out of the cubicle and down the hall, barefoot, the bib still pinned on me, pockets of foam still on my face. The girl wipes off the foam with a clean hot towel, another girl puts on my socks and shoes, and the soldier waits as I pay them and tip them—for the life of me I have no idea whether I am paying too much or too little. I think I handed her the equivalent of a twelve-dollar bill. The barber reads his sports magazine as though nothing has happened.

"Pally, pally," the soldier says, "Quickly, quickly." He leads the way down the steep narrow stairway. Outside there are several other Korean soldiers sitting in, or standing around, a jeep, their characteristically stony countenances turning to amusement at the sight of me.

"What's happening?" I ask.

"Be quiet," the one next to the driver answers me in English, and the one behind him in the jeep says, "We have to decide what to do with him. . . ."

A taxi comes along and one of them hails it. He explains to

the driver where they think I want to go. The monsoon rains have yet to arrive, though the night has grown more humid, if a bit cooler than the daytime. As I climb into the back seat of the cab, I simply nod good night to them. They nod back.

As the cabbie drives over the Third Han River Bridge, I say, "Looks like we're going to have some weather."

For a second, I imagine he is going to turn around and say, *"Dog Soldiers,* right? I read that." But it's clear from his expression that he hasn't the faintest idea what I am talking about. He drives through the Nam San tunnel, through the downtown streets, less crowded now, and heads up Sejong-ro. He turns right at Kwanghwamun Gate, makes a left near the palace grounds, and, just before the Blue House entrance, hangs a right onto the winding upgrade of Samchung-dong.

TEA
AT THE
PALAZ
OF HOON

Mr. Han designs houses. He works with an architect on his sketches and ideas, then he builds. But he involves himself in more than floor plans; he travels to Tokyo and Hong Kong, Brussels and New York, ostensibly on business, but also to walk and window-shop, searching for light-fixtures, tiles, a transom, or doorknobs. He worries about every detail, down to the appliances in the kitchen, the furniture in the living room, the artwork on the walls, and the bathroom faucets. Finding the right stones for a garden, a persimmon tree of the perfect shape, a dwarf maple of the proper delicacy, and azalea bushes that will bloom a particular color in spring—any of such projects consumes him for months on end.

Since our arrival a week ago, he has finished work on a large embassy residence up the hill, and now is involved with a house over the south wall of the garden, a home for Mrs. Han's son, Hae-Chul, when he returns from France at the end of the summer.

Haeja still has jet lag, but Fionna has taken to her new surroundings wonderfully, and I've gotten into the flow of Seoul's rhythm within a few days. Each morning I get up before sunrise, stretch, then go to the park up the road to work out and run. When I return, sometimes I stop near the embassy residence, which has yet to be occupied, and walk around its garden, listening to the waterfall running over the stone grotto that Mr. Han designed. I go up a hill to Sunrise Rock and watch the first light come over the distant eastern mountain range, and on the way back home I visit the new construction site, where Mr. Han is usually already busy with his foreman, Mr. Yun, and the workmen.

This morning the workers are busy hauling bricks in wheelbarrows, removing boulders, and then lugging in stones for the garden. Yesterday morning Mr. Han identified some of the new stones: flatrock from the Han River, pink crystal-veined rock from Okchon, perforated sea rock from Cholla-do.

I don't yet know much about Mr. Han, a tall, youthful, middle-aged man given to quietness and even great silences. He is not a brooder, though; the lapses in his conversations are those of a thinker, an aesthete, a problem-solver. Though he seems detached from Seoul's social world, he takes great satisfaction in his family and work; and while he isn't spontaneous, his energy and vitality seems considered. Within the family he is highly regarded and engaging. Mr. Han dresses in a casual, sporty way, but his composure is all Confucian.

Everything I've heard about him is from Haeja, and she herself knows little about her stepfather, because she did not live with her parents and she met Mr. Han only a few times before coming to America ten years ago. He was, in her childish mind, this shadowy figure who came to visit her mother, the children forbidden to go to the rooms upstairs when he visited their house. Eventually, Haeja's mother would move in with Mr. Han. Shortly after that, her mother had one more child and then another. Haeja would learn years later that her stepfather had three other children himself, and when he set up a new household with her mother, his ex-wife would have custody of those children for the next twelve years; eventually, though, his children and the two children he had with Haeja's mother would live in the old restored house on Samchung-dong.

Divorce was an uneasy institution in Korea, or at least it still was unconventional after the Korean War, so that the Hans were looked at critically by relatives and friends. Mr. Han was always accorded a great deal of respect by his own children, but they, like children of divorce anywhere, had resentments and misunderstandings. Some of the children got along with the new Mrs. Han better than they did with him. One child didn't seem to get along with any parent and so lived with Haeja's brother, sister, and grandmother, away from his imme-diate family. Haeja had left Korea when she was a teenager, and so she did not really know some of her stepbrothers and stepsisters, her half brother and half sister all that well. Com-pared with other men in his generation, Haeja told me, her stepfather was a very kind, considerate, and open-minded per-son. He was well educated, artistic, even slightly bohemian, and eccentric. In a world of black-market swindlers, politicians with military backgrounds, and trauma victims of a bloody war, Mr. Han attempted to create an oasis of tranquillity with three different families under one roof. Though not all of his children could be persuaded, he and Mrs. Han wanted each of them to consider the house a place of harmony, without divisions, without recriminations. To a great extent, Mr. Han, with his wife's help, had succeeded in this virtually impossible task.

Over the years, I had heard many stories about Haeja's mother, but not very much about Mr. Han. I knew that he was the scion of an old family fortune and that his family's history was synonymous with that of Korea over the past five hundred years during its last and longest dynasty, the Yi. Had the country not been annexed by the Japanese shortly after the beginning of this century, Mr. Han would have been not only a nobleman but a prince. Yet, Haeja used to tell me, he was a modest man, very down-to-earth, a practical man, making his own separate peace with the tumultuous world of postwar Korea.

The ancient names of Korea come to mind. Choson: Morning Calm. Koryo: High and Sparkling Land. The Three Kingdoms: Koguryo, Paekche, Silla. Puyo: a mythological time when Tangun, the bear king, ruled.

During the time of the Three Kingdoms, Korea stretched beyond the geographical boundaries of its peninsula into Manchuria, the northernmost kingdom with cultural and social customs similar to those of the Altaic tribes that spread across Asia into Europe. Before the Yi and Koryo dynasties, the peninsula's great dynasty—and one of its greatest cultures—came from Silla in the southernmost provinces. Silla was at its peak in the seventh century, eventually giving way over the centuries to Koryo, which set up a new capital in Kaesong at the present Demilitarized Zone that divides North and South Korea. After the end of this dynasty in the late fourteenth century, the Yi dynasty came into power and moved the capital once again, this time to Seoul. Starting in the 1390s, the Yi lasted over five hundred years until 1910, when Japan annexed the country and eliminated the royalty.

Although the Japanese invaded Korea several times during the Yi dynasty, the greatest influence on Korea through its dynastic periods was the generally benign one exerted by China. Korea used Chinese characters in its writing, and Chinese thought and customs pervaded its daily life. Back in the time of the Three Kingdoms, Buddhism first came to Korea as a way of appeasing the rulers of China, where the religion flourished. During the Silla dynasty, T'ang painting influenced its arts, and by the late Koryo dynasty and throughout the Yi dynasty, neo-Confucian thought was the cornerstone of Korean civilization.

On my first day in Seoul, Mr. Han gave me a tour of the house, explaining how it was restored about a decade after the war. As we walked through the rooms I saw not so much a place as a kind of biography of a man, especially in the smaller objects that decorated the rooms. Three of these objects—a blue and white bowl, a photograph, and a Chinese calligraphic painting—embodied not only a history of the house and its inhabitants but even a personal history of Korea.

The calligraphic painting—showing the character for a plum blossom—belonged to Han Myung-Hoon (a *yangban,* or nobleman) in the court of the first Yi dynasty king, T'aejo. Late in the fourteenth century, General Yi conquered the Koryo dynasty and moved the capital from Kaesong, at the present DMZ, to Seoul, changing the manner of the country from a Buddhist to a neo-Confucian one. The newly appointed king made Han a minister in his government. He deeded the new minister a parcel of land north of the palace grounds, the property where I stand right now.

The photograph in the black frame is that of another government minister, Mr. Han's grandfather Han Sul-Hoon, an adviser to the last Yi king, just before the Japanese annexed the country, around the turn of the century, five hundred years after his ancestors first settled in Seoul.

An enlightened man, Han Sul-Hoon believed in progress, modernization, even westernization. Minister Han had always had a love of learning and the sense that progress would bring a better future. His father had made him travel widely before settling down to his government position in Seoul during the years of Japanese rule. His ideas endeared him to some Koreans and to many Japanese who had similar ideas, but these ideas also made him a figure of mistrust for other countrymen, who called him a collaborator.

In keeping with his ideas of progress, Han Sul-Hoon sent his own son, Mr. Han's father, Kyung-Hoon, abroad to study, first at Cambridge University, where he took a degree, and then on to graduate school at Johns Hopkins University in Baltimore.

When Mr. Han's father returned to Korea, he started the country's first bank and bought up huge tracts of land, especially in and around Seoul. The year before his son's birth, the original house burned to the ground. It was rebuilt in the old style, with joints fitted together without nails. Up until a few years ago, the property spread out in all directions. From the years in England, his father had acquired a love of dogs, particularly British terriers, so Mr. Han grew up surrounded by dogs—"maybe forty of them," he said—and countless household servants.

It was his father's ambition that Mr. Han study abroad, like himself, and then come back to run the family enterprises. But Mr. Han had always wanted to be an architect, a love he acquired from his grandfather, who taught him about the ancient buildings in and around their land. The father's plans for his son were thwarted by World War II and the Japanese

41

occupation. Instead of studying abroad, Mr. Han studied in Seoul. Instead of becoming a businessman or even a licensed architect, he became a brilliant amateur designer, a professional builder, a realtor, and a connoisseur of Korean folk art.

As was the custom for wealthy men of his day, Mr. Han's father had five wives, and the younger Han's mother was Japanese. At the outbreak of the Korean War, Mr. Han was in Tokyo, visiting her, and he did not return to Seoul until the cease-fire three years later.

When the Korean War broke out, Mr. Han told me, his father was the first so-called capitalist dog that the Communists murdered. His thousands of western books, purchased over his student years in Cambridge and Baltimore, were used as toilet paper by the North Korean military that commandeered the house as a headquarters after first capturing Seoul in the summer of 1950. Through several occupations, the house would become a Communist and later a UN headquarters, and later still an American hospital dispensary.

By then the family home was in ruins, and now all that is left are details of the woodwork, windows, floors, and walls. It would take ten more years before Mr. Han could begin to rebuild the house with Haeja's mother, a process that continues to this day.

When I come to the work site, Mr. Han is in the process of laying a pattern on the ground for the workmen to follow as they place the various elements of the rock garden—river stones, pink marble, the organic granite shapes, and the perforated stones like those in Asian folk-painting landscapes.

New trees lie on their sides awaiting planting, the largest a pear tree whose roots are swathed in burlap and secured by hemp rope.

Neatly dressed in sport shirt and casual pants, Mr. Han kneels on the sodden ground, creating circular patterns with a rope he pivots from a stick. His purposeful demeanor reminds me of how Jackson Pollock might have worked on a painting. The workers strike me as being not so much artists as geomancers. Mr. Han sculpts while they divine.

The garden needs an organic shape not only to complement the terrain, but also to appease the resident spirits, nearby mountain gods as well as ancestors from the Han clan who spent centuries in this locale. Koreans are Confucians socially, Buddhists when times are difficult, but they are animists nearly always. Even in the short time I've known Mr. Han, I've surmised that his practicality is leavened by intuition and a proper humility toward the ancestors.

I sit on a mound of dirt, take off my soaked T-shirt, and light up a cigarette. Mr. Han stops what he is doing and comes over. "You can't walk around without a shirt," he says good-naturedly. "You had better put it back on."

Mr. Han is a liberal man surrounded by martinets, a thinker in a world of soldiers and ex-generals. He is also a fellow artist, so I don't take his admonition as a slight. I put my shirt back on.

On the west of the construction site is a green cyclone fence, the boundary of the Blue House, the presidential grounds. Several elite guards in camouflage fatigues, automatic weapons in their hands, stand looking over the fence at us. One of them carries a field radio on his back and gets on the horn to check in.

When they go back up the hill, Mr. Han says, "You must be careful who you speak with. And you must be careful what you say to everyone, even inside the house."

The expression on his face changes from gravity to pleasure in an instant as he points to the future rock garden.

"Good design is very simple."

He puffs on his cigarette, then stubs it out.

"Very simple," he repeats, drifting off. "Resolve yourself here. Use it well."

One of the workers approaches Mr. Han with a roof tile unearthed in the excavation that is probably from the original summer palace. Mr. Han turns the tile in his hand, then hands it to me; I turn it in my own hands, over and over, examining the Bodhidarmalike face chiseled into it. I realize that the oldest possession I have is a broken Timex watch from high school, my oldest memory is as a four-year-old boy in Brooklyn (my birthday party, dressed as Hopalong Cassidy, several months before the outbreak of the Korean War). My mother's family goes back a hundred and fifty years in Brooklyn, and before that to Albany, New York, and to Belfast, Ireland. My father is shanty Irish from the west coast of Ireland, Clare and Mayo, the Gaeltecht. But my roots really go back to Moon Mullins, Smokey Stover, and Popeye. Instead of Dharma bums from roof tiles, there are wooden rosary beads from Assisi, brown scapulars from churches in Brooklyn, memories of "The Honeymooners," youth gangs in front of candy stores, Spaldeen high-bouncers, stickball bats, and stoops in hot summers in East New York.

"Let's have breakfast," Mr. Han says, walking off toward the house.

We enter the house down a long alley to the back door, where we remove our shoes and come into a large modern kitchen, off of which there are many smaller bedrooms. But the center of the house is the living room, which still retains the long, rectangular shape of hundreds of years, although electricity, central heating, and air-conditioning have been added. The spare furniture of ancestors has been superseded by big western couches and easy chairs, and Chinese rugs partially cover the polished, dark wood floors.

Haeja had long talked about her parents' living in "a palace," which conjured up pictures in my mind ranging from Jefferson's Monticello to the villas in Matisse's paintings. But now I see that this "palace" is of a very human scale, a tasteful, elegant home that seamlessly combines new and old. If anything, it reminds me most of Green and Green's California bungalows around the turn of the century. The beauty of the architecture is found in the shades and tones of the various woods, the scope of the minutest details like doorknobs and windowpanes, and the concern for comfort and habitation in livable proportions.

The walls are filled with Korean folk paintings, the bookshelves with pottery from the major Korean dynasties, primitive comb-marked, dirt-colored vases from seventh-century Silla, celadons from Koryo a thousand years ago, and white porcelains from the Yi period. A clay roof tile is mounted in a windowsill, wooden ceremonial ducks and horn boxes ornament the Korean chests, and on one wall, a large screen is opened out, depicting a royal scene at the palace, thousands of tiny figures minutely rendered.

At the west end of the room the ceiling is vaulted, supported by thick, amber-colored wood pillars, the rough beams in the ceiling exposed. I am told that this peak is where the *chip shin ryung,* household spirits, reside. Korea's equivalent of the Furies, they are chthonic goddesses who gave up the wildness of the earth for domesticity.

All the rooms of the house seem to flow from this central

one. The room itself looks out onto a bank of sliding glass doors facing the garden, which once encompassed land as far as the eye could see, but over time the property has been reduced to about a quarter acre that is bordered by a traditional wall of large, squarish granite bricks topped by inverted half-moons of slate tile.

The bedrooms have rich, straw-colored floors made of rice paper and bean oil, and heat rises up from them. At night, mats are rolled out onto these *ondol* floors. Since Haeja and I sleep in the study, a room without this type of heating, a western-style bed has been placed there. When I first arrived, I set up my typewriter at a little desk in the study, and now everyone in the family jokingly refers to the room as the *sarang-bang.* In olden days the *sarang-bang* was the scholar's quarters, which stood separate from the main house and it was there that the men went to read, write, smoke, drink wine, and be entertained.

Besides the Hans and ourselves, four of the eight children still live here as well as four or five maids and, out back in a cottage, a houseman. At the base of the hill there is a gatehouse for Mr. Yun, the foreman, and across the street on Samchung-dong, Mr. Paik, the driver, lives with his family. With the exception of Hae-Chul in Europe and Haeja in America, the entire family lives in Chongro-ku, this northern neighborhood in the old part of Seoul.

After a shower and a shave, I dress and cross the living room to the few steps leading down into the kitchen. This is the second largest room in the house, and in the morning the most active one. A few of the *ajima*, the maids (literally "aunties"), are preparing breakfast or beginning on lunch and even dinner. The others gather clothing to be washed or mop the floors with a cloth, squatting on their haunches or bent over like farmers planting rice seedlings in springtime.

Every day an ajima comes into the study to collect clothes to be washed; every other day, to replace the linen. She takes the laundry to a machine in the kitchen, then hangs it out on a line in a brick courtyard behind the house, near the giant earth-colored urns that contain the family supply of *kim-chee,* the spicy, pickled cabbage served at every meal, *ko-choo chang,* hot pepper sauce, and *doeng-jhang,* a brownish bean paste. In an American household, domestic help might seem almost extraneous to the overall rhythm of the household, but Korean ajima are an integral part of the family. Most of these maids have been with Mrs. Han since she was a young woman. The brighter ones have become her assistants, some eventually even friends and intimates. And because of their sheer numbers, each helps another, so that no one does backbreaking work alone.

Mr. Han is finicky about his lunch and dinner, and often he prefers to eat out at a restaurant downtown, but in the morning his tastes are simple: for breakfast he has a cup of coffee and a bowl of *udong,* noodles, with a raw egg broken over the top. When I come into the kitchen, he is seated already, the ajima bustling around to get his meal. Today I ask to join him in a bowl of udong instead of my usual American breakfast. Nearly every morning this past week I have had a glass of Andy-Boy orange juice with its tinny aftertaste, one or two eggs over light, several pieces of ersatz Wonderbread from a hotel downtown, and instant coffee with nondairy creamer. All around the low table there are tiny celadon bowls filled with jelly, pats of butter, and, because Mrs. Han had heard I liked it, Peter Pan peanut butter. Along with this fare, the ajima serve sides of thick fresh bacon and what they call "sausage," American hot dogs.

The ajima debate among themselves whether I want simply udong or udong with a raw egg, so I tell them that I want udong with raw egg, please—the way Mr. Han has his.

The noodles arrive in a large Chinese bowl, next to it a small celadon bowl containing the egg, which I ceremoniously break over the top of the steaming noodles while everyone watches. Even Mrs. Han, already engaged on the telephone doing business, pauses to watch. I eat, using chopsticks and silver spoon just as Mr. Han does. But the kitchen ladies stare at me, as though something is wrong, and so does Mr. Han.

"Don't you like their noodles?" he finally asks.

"They're delicious," I exclaim.

"But you are so quiet, Michael. You must make some noise with your noodles or they will think you don't like the food."

Mr. Han demonstrates, sucking into his open mouth a mound of raw egg and noodles with loud slurps, *Ah!*

Following his example, I slurp loudly, sigh, say *Ah!* It is as if a spell has been removed from the kitchen ladies, for now they resume moving around, talking, and laughing. Mrs. Han goes back to her telephone conversation. Mr. Han polishes off the remainder of his noodles. It crosses my mind that my own father would have whacked me on the head and sent me from the table for such lack of manners.

The noodles cleared away, everyone leaves the low table to attend to other work. Friends and relatives often stop by at this hour—unannounced, as is the custom in Seoul. More often than not, Mrs. Han deals with these visitors, leaving Mr. Han free to do his work on the house next door. Today, I stay at the low table in the kitchen, smoking a cigarette and drinking a cup of instant coffee. Sometimes one of the Hans' daughters,

Byung-Soon and Byung-Ju, stops for a bite before bustling off to classes at the university, or Byung-Jeen, the Hans' oldest son, comes to the table for a leisurely, late meal—he has completed college and all that remains before he begins his career are a few months that he must commit to the military reserves. But this morning no one comes into the kitchen, and I go off to the study to do some reading and writing.

When I emerge, Mr. Han is in the living room, finishing up yet another of his domestic ceremonies, a set of yoga exercises he performs several times a day. Though he is in his fifties, he is in very good shape, and he looks ten or fifteen years younger than his age.

He rolls up the exercise mat and puts it in a corner, then stands looking at a new painting by Kim Hong-do, a legendary Yi folk artist who went by the name Tanwon. Mr. Han is contemplating buying it.

The painting shows a man hiking up a mountain, searching for roots and carrying a sack over his shoulder and a hoe in his hand; the look on his face is that of one spellbound by nature. Below him, a deer stops under a blossoming apple tree and looks up, surprised at the human notice. The eyes of the deer and the man are black dots, simple yet full of emotion and wonder, and the painting gives me the feeling I get when I come on a Rembrandt portrait; I'm startled by how contemporary the face and expression are.

"What do you think?" asks Mr. Han.

He studies the painting carefully, steps back not only to admire it but to assay it coolly. Is it real? And if so, is it a good example?

"It's very nice," I say. "Just lovely. Even grand."

Mr. Han lights a cigarette and studies the painting further.

"Good quality." He nods.

I'm not sure if I'm supposed to offer a further opinion or simply be quiet and study the painting as Mr. Han is doing. What he studies, what he is looking for, is clear to him—he is an authority about this kind of artwork. I admit to him that I am only halfway through a book on Yi dynasty folk paintings, one of several books on Korean art in his library.

"That's not important," he says.

"That's true," I agree, "but all I can do is admire the painting in a very superficial way. I'm not sure of its significance—or how I would compare this painting, say, to another of Tan-won's at the National Museum. . . ."

"No, no, no, no," Mr. Han says, laughing, but sounding a bit exasperated by his American son-in-law. "None of that is necessary for looking at art." He struggles to find the words in English for what he wants to say. "You simply look—there!—you can tell right away if it is working well or not. . . ."

Mrs. Han joins us, nodding her head with great approval.

"How can you tell if it is good?" I ask her.

"How?" She looks to Mr. Han as if confused.

He laughs and lights a cigarette, and I light one, too. Both of them look at me oddly, in the way that Mr. Han looked at me when I took off my shirt. He laughs again.

"In America," he asks, "do you always smoke in front of elders?" I'm not sure what he means. I have presumed, since he smokes, that my smoking does not bother him.

Then he says, "Here in Korea, it is very impolite—it is not done—to smoke in front of an older person." I snuff out the cigarette. "Of course, I don't mind," he says. "I just thought you should know."

Mrs. Han joins in the discussion.

"Father means that it looks bad if you smoke in front of him, even if personally he does not mind. People will think that you don't respect him."

"Oh, but I do respect you, sir," I say defensively.

This distinction—Mr. Han doesn't mind if I smoke in front of him, but would look bad if he permitted it—is not so different from those an American might make; his acceptance of this protocol, combined with its strangeness to me, make it seem somehow immutable.

"If you must smoke when I am around," he says, "please do it when no one else is here."

A sudden explosion stops the conversation. The windows rattle, the floor buckles, the air seems to be sucked out of the room. Every day, and sometimes twice a day since I arrived this has happened. I have been told it is some kind of test, but no one seems to know exactly what kind or where. I take it as a sign of my having become acclimatized to Seoul that this time I don't bother to ask what is happening. But Mrs. Han looks rattled and goes off to her room.

Mr. Han settles into one of the easy chairs, listening to his Chinese-language tapes in preparation for a trip to Hong Kong that he plans to make in the fall. Byung-Jeen joins us; sitting on the couch, he begins reading a book on strategies for *paduk*, the game of Go. Byung-Chul, the youngest son, comes in, too, this being Sunday; on school days I never see him, because when he is not in high school attending classes, he is out being tutored until midnight curfew. Byung-Soon and Byung-Ju come in; they are eager to practice English, but too shy to approach me yet.

I have come to realize how rare it is for the entire household to be at home and more or less at leisure. There really is no such thing as a day of rest in Korea; people work seven days a week, sixteen- to eighteen-hour days, 360 or so days a year. They may take off for the New Year and one or two other days, the more affluent people for perhaps a few days' vacation in the summer.

A minute later the calm is broken once again, this time by Mr. Paik, the driver, who points and gestures wildly, and exits with the entire family in tow.

One of the few neighbors on this private street is a general in the military government, and it appears that he has chopped down one of the Hans' dwarf maple trees in order to widen his own driveway so he won't have to leave his car on the street.

For many years the Hans have had trouble with this neighbor and other figures in the military government because of their proximity to the Blue House. The military has made many attempts to buy the surrounding properties. Once, many years ago, they even took the Hans in "for questioning," not about any specific improprieties on their part, but simply to nudge them—"to shoulder them," as Haeja said—into having an interest in selling. Even the government could not confiscate the property outright, but were the Hans to be remiss on their property taxes, for example. . . .

The other morning on my run, I had come on the tree-chopping neighbor. He looked baffled as to how an American had come to be in this restricted area. He had a ruddy face, a bull-like neck, and a stocky, broad-shouldered frame, low to the ground, immediately bringing to mind a tank and also the Mother Superior who ruled the grade school I attended. To her, there was only one way to do anything—hers! But whereas her power resided in the triangular ruler with which she tapped the palm of her left hand, his power lay in his uniform, heavily ribboned and studded with medals, with lots of scrambled eggs on the brim of his hat. His two bodyguards, and especially the

sawed-off automatic weapon one carried at hip level, rein-
forced the image.

With everyone in the household busy attending to this new
ripple in their relationship with their neighbor, I have the
house and its treasures to myself in the early afternoon.

I slide open a glass door in the living room, step out into the
garden. Purple azaleas blossom, and the dwarf maple leaves are
a delicate red. Forsythia explode the last of their yellow color.
A squirrel runs up a big oak tree. A magpie alights on the wall,
and a giant black butterfly floats by. (Some days I see a pheas-
ant strutting in the garden, but not today.) A stray cat chases
the squirrel up an oak tree. I see workmen pass by the elabo-
rately ornamental wrought-iron gate. There, facing me in the
garden, are two squat protectors against fire, stone dragons that
seem to leer and fume. Occasionally, the back door swings
open; an ajima comes out, takes the lid off a gigantic urn, dips
a ladle in, and scoops a dollop of hot pepper paste into a bowl,
then goes back into the kitchen. Another ajima comes out with
a pot in her hands, goes over to the well in a stone grotto on
the hillside behind a terrace and draws some spring water for
cooking.

I look back to the house, taking in the curved tiles on the
ancient roof, the gargoyle rainspouts, the newer western wing,
where the bedrooms and the kitchen are, and the Hans' bedroom jutting out into the garden. The doors open onto a delicate wooden balcony, the *maru,* where I see Mrs. Han talking
with someone.

When they come out to the garden, the man, sporting a
business suit and a big, ingratiating smile, has his hand extended even before we are introduced.

"Michael," he shouts, "it is a great pleasure." He pumps my hand vigorously, smiling all the time, and I assume he is one of Haeja's cousins, though he looks maybe ten years older than I am and is probably ten years younger than Mrs. Han.

"This is Mr. Mo," Mrs. Han says finally.

The name is not one I am familiar with.

"Call me Uncle Mo," says the beaming gentleman. "Your mother-in-law and I are distant relatives from Taegu."

"We're not related," Mrs. Han says quickly.

"Very distantly," Uncle Mo beams, not missing a beat or losing his smile.

"His mother would help my mother occasionally," Mrs. Han clarifies.

"Distant relatives," he laughs. "Like I said." His English is quite good, yet he does not seem to be a man of the Hans' social position—an important distinction that I'm learning to discern.

"Well, we have work," says Mrs. Han, impatient to leave. "Mr. Mo is to speak with our neighbor."

"Let's get together," Uncle Mo says. "Do you play golf?"

"He doesn't play golf," Mrs. Han says. "He's a writer."

"I used to," I say as they head off.

"Then let's get together," calls Uncle Mo. "I rarely have a chance to practice my English."

Later, I learn that Uncle Mo is a kind of Mr. Fixit with the military government. A former officer, he has many associates from his military days in the government. If the maple-tree incident is to be resolved, Uncle is the man to get the job done.

In the late afternoon Haeja talks with her mother in the kitchen as Fionna takes a nap, and Mr. Han invites me into his bedroom to look at a screen he has opened out on the wall behind his sleeping mat. I am braced for a second explosion, which usually occurs around this time of day.

The screen is a *chekkori,* a book painting, my favorite genre of Korean art. Symbols of the Confucian esteem for scholars, a set of these paintings would hang in the sarang-bang of a traditional house. Their design reminds me of cubist paintings, their dominant image simply stacks of books, piled on their sides and standing together, accompanied by objects associated with scholars—a pipe, a brush and pen, an inkstone, a cup. The darker ones remind me of Braque; the lighter, more buoyant ones have goldfish floating in the air along with pocket watches, and remind me of Dada and Surrealism (Western styles of art that later Korean folk artists were aware of, even influenced by).

An ajima comes to say that Mr. Han is wanted out back by his foreman, concerning the maple tree. Alone in the room, I look at the new screen, and then at the room itself, where I rarely go except to summon Fionna, who comes here constantly in search of candy. The room is spare and elegant, with its ondol floor, the sliding doors opening onto the delicate maru balcony, and another set of sliding doors leading to the hallway and the sliding doors on the other side of the hall, facing the garden. Besides the two bed mats on the floor, there is a persimmon-wood chest, and a long, low, lacquered side table where the overly ornamental old-fashioned telephone is placed along with a bunch of invitations to dinner parties, gallery openings, and embassy lunches. Several of them, I notice, are addressed to Prince Han. When Mr. Han returns, I ask him about the title. I know he is not an Yi, and even if he were, Korea is no longer a monarchy.

"A distant relation to a queen," he says dismissively, light-

55

ing a cigarette, and adds that such a relationship does not count for much in Confucian society.

"This was the summer palace," I say.

"One of them," he states, blowing out smoke.

"Your family's house?" I ask.

"A royal summer house," he clarifies, and turns back to the screen. When he looks my way, he notices that I am still musing over the invitations.

"The queen had many such houses as this," Mr. Han says.

"And your family was her family," I venture.

"She had many such relatives as us," he laughs. I can see that he has reached the end of this particular conversation. With a sly look at me, he says, "Americans are very interested in royal families, it seems."

"I was only asking," I say, thrown off guard.

"Ah, ah," he puffs on his cigarette, "only asking, I see. . . ." And with that, he walks out of the room, leaving me to ponder the goldfish in the air, the pocket watches floating in the clouds, the stacks of books in the screen, and the invitations pinned to the mirror.

When you drink tea at the Palaz of Hoon, this is how the world appears, sometimes upside down, sometimes as an anachronism. Invitations are addressed to princes; neighbors are squat generals bent on axing your maple trees. When the moon rises over Korea, a stream of fish, octupi, medusas, sea-shells, and crabs arc through the sky, their skins and carapaces the color of amber. Behind them come the spirits of rivers and mountains, trees and rocks, the men who drowned in streams and turned into carp but now are transformed after millennia into dragons. Because the moon is a woman, it is accompanied by the sun, her man, and deer, tortoise, and magpie arc through the night sky in a stream of peach flowers and branches, the borders of the amber sky turning an auspicious red, which all sailors know is a good sign. With the dead souls of the Earth are the heavenly ones like Tangun, who is followed by a file of tigers and bears, and they in turn are followed by oxen, river dragons, foxes, snakes, more deer, and rabbits. The sky takes on the color of an amber light, the color of wheat, the granite mountains, the ondol floor, and the moon itself. The borders of the sky turn red like the weather in a sailor's dream.

GRANDMA
OH

할머니

As we go around the side of the house, a maid comes out the back door with an aluminum pot and scoops out kochoo-chang, hot bean paste, from one of the many large, dark brown urns on the terrace out back. The ajima smiles hello to us, humming a song under her breath, and scurries back into the kitchen. Haeja and I leave by the back-alley entrance. Six-foot walls, topped by curved tiles, line both sides of the narrow, isolated lane. The only homes on this cul-de-sac are the Hans' old house and three or four modern residences. Although it is only minutes from downtown Seoul, trees are everywhere, Samchung Mountain looms up behind the houses—and the rhythm is nearly pastoral.

Chongro-ku was once the center of the city. Now Seoul spreads out in every direction, but especially in the south below the Han River, an area known as New Seoul.

58

Because of the proximity of the palace grounds and the presidential mansion, the neighborhood has a quality of the exclusive and the *verboten,* imperial and martial. But unlike the elite neighborhoods of other cities, Seoul is a hodgepodge where the wealthy, the middle class, and the poor live side by side, and Samchung-dong is no exception. As Korea becomes a nation of consumers, the differences between rich and poor surface most obviously in cars, clothing, and purchasing power in general. Yet the degrees of difference between rich and poor are mostly subtle ones, having to do primarily with duty and responsibility, and especially with a sense of class so powerful it nearly amounts to a caste system. Still, rich and poor share certain values and customs, and though a wealthy person's home may be larger than his poor neighbor's, what goes on socially and culturally in both abodes is in many ways similar.

Up and down the hillsides, and at street level—even directly across from the gate to the presidential mansion—there are shantylike dwellings of the very poor, often only one or two rooms. Interspersed among them are the older, more traditional two-room structures of the working class and the lower-middle class, which often lack heat and running water, and have only makeshift kitchens and little space.

Samchung-dong is a narrow, winding, ascending street. The mountain—a bald granite rock face, parts of which are covered with pines and evergreens—looms in the background.

Lining the west side of the street are a row of small shops: a greengrocer, a fishmonger's stall, a bridal shop, a furniture store specializing in rattan, the police station, a pharmacy, a mom-and-pop candy and cigarette store, and one or two small restaurants. On the east side of the street tiny one- or two-room houses work their way up the side of yet another hillside;

the maze of cobbled byways between them is too narrow and steep for cars.

At this time of day, groups of old men walk up and down along Samchung-dong, going to or coming back from their exercise. They wear traditional Yi dress, pastel-colored baggy silk pants with billowing shirts and loose-fitting vests, rubber shoes, and horsehair hats. Some of them have goatees; some smoke long pipes. Others dress more casually, in slacks and penny loafers and short-sleeved white shirts. Nearly all of them wear eyeglasses and carry walking sticks or canes; they speak loudly, maybe because of deafness. One or two sing old songs. Because age is revered in Confucian and Taoist societies, not one has that air of lost youth that elderly Americans some-times project. In many respects, they are men in the prime of their lives, free from the burden of work, esteemed, and well cared for.

The sight of these old men reminds me of where we are going—to visit Grandma Oh, who lives at the Lees' house.

We turn just before the entrance to the park and walk up a steep, winding hill. At the top is the abandoned Vietnamese embassy with its elaborate Chinese-style gate.

Across the street, a unit of cadets marches down the moun-tain road, lockstep ten across and ten deep, their fatigues im-maculately pressed. They chant to a marching-drill cadence, proceeding into the parking lot of an official-looking building. Knots of sweetpea blossoms are entwined in a wall along the side of the road. Haeja has the purposeful look of Little Red Riding Hood on her way to Grandma's house.

The top of the hill flattens out, then winds down into Kao-hai-dong. We pass Songgyun'gwan University, one of the old-est academic institutions in Korea; outside the rear entrance, riot police with clubs and plastic shields lounge around a green armored vehicle of prehistoric-looking, armadillolike construction. The slightest aroma of tear gas tinges the air.

The Lees' house sits at the edge of a quiet, winding, hilly lane, its courtyard surrounded by a brick wall with Korean tiles on top. These tiny houses honeycomb the hillsides, filling up the lanes off this street. Cobbled together with bricks and mortar, most of them were built during the Yi dynasty and the years of Japanese occupation in this century; they disappeared or were ruined during the Korean War, and were rebuilt.

We walk down the narrow lane to the Lees' old house, and knock on the door. An old woman no taller than four and a half feet opens the door and laughs. *"Aigo,* it's Haeja." She lets out another hoarse, wheezy laugh, waves to us shyly, almost like a little girl, and immediately comes toward me, laughing, coughing, shaking my hand. *"Aigo,"* she says, "it's Michael *Sa-bong."* Michael-the-husband. So tall, she says, "just like a chopstick."

"Aigo," Grandma Oh says, "I am too old when I see Haeja a mother and wife."

Everyone calls Grandma Oh "Halmoni"—Kao-hai-dong Halmoni, actually, after the street she lives on. Halmoni pats her granddaughter, squeezes her arms, hugs her. She gestures for us to come in, come in, and pats me on the back good-naturedly. There is not a moment's hesitation in her greeting, even though I am probably the first American she has encountered socially in her long life.

Grandma Oh wears a gray hanbok, the traditional Yi dynasty dress, but the color has bleached out and faded to an off-white. Her face is so withered that it seems ageless; the wrinkles on her face are a map, or tell a story.

"So tall," she says again, laughing. "They must have good kim-chee in Mi-Guk." Mi-Guk is the United States.

"Quickly, quickly," she says.

We step inside the small courtyard of this traditionally structured house, and other members of the family wander out. There are Hae-Soon, Haeja's older sister, her husband, Mr. Lee, and their three children. Behind them stand three old ajima, more companions for Grandma Oh than Hae-Soon's helpers.

She lights another cigarette and coughs, then laughs and shakes my hand again. She motions for us to go up the concrete steps into the living room.

"Aaiiigggoo, Haeja-ga is back home." Halmoni pulls on my arm, and I follow her up three big concrete steps into the living room.

"Michael Sa-bong," she says, chuckling.

All around the little courtyard there are tiny rooms. I feel as though I have stepped into a dollhouse. The doors slide open, their bottoms a thin blond wood, their upper portions panes of glass. The rooms are built on a high concrete foundation, and each rooftop is made of tubular slate tiles arrayed in comblike patterns. The eaves' edges curl upward airily in that way common throughout Asia; I once heard this is the architectural influence of the Mongols' tents.

The sky above is a heavenly azure this beautiful June day.

I had heard Haeja tell so many stories about her grandmother that I probably knew more about her than anyone else in the family: for five years I've carried around a thumbnail portrait of Grandma Oh in my mind, and now I try to locate the biography in this tiny, frail yet energetic woman, with a face so old that it seems to encompass several lifetimes.

The year that she was born, her father joined a native revolt against the Japanese, who had forced the Korean nobles to shave their topknots. The year before, the great matriarch

Queen Min had been assassinated by Japanese gangsters. Shortly into the new century, war broke out between Russia and Japan on Korean soil. When she was ten the country had become a protectorate under Japan, and the year before her arranged marriage at sixteen the Japanese annexed the country.

Her father was a yangban, a noble landowner, in the city of Taegu in Kyong-Sang Province, and it was he who sent Grandma Oh's husband to Seoul to study. The husband came back a few years later, cultured and refined, only to get her pregnant, teach her to smoke a long pipe, and then leave her for good, going off with a so-called new woman, one with city ways and sophistication. Alone, she raised her son Pyong-Hoon, who would in turn grow up and go off to Tokyo to study medicine.

We are staying at the Hans' house on the other side of the mountain, but I can tell by the expression on Haeja's face that any house in Seoul where her older sister and grandmother live is home. At her mother's house she is a kind of black sheep, the prodigal daughter who ran off to America. Here, she is still just Haeja, the baby sister and the girl her grandmother raised.

"How long?" asks Grandma Oh. "How many years?"

"A long time," Haeja says. "Ten years."

"How is your singing? Are you still singing? You had a beautiful voice, always a beautiful voice."

"I still give concerts," Haeja says, "but I'm not singing enough. Raising a child takes so much work."

Grandma Oh nods knowingly. Tell me about it, her face seems to say. Almost instantly, she sits Haeja down, then slides down onto the floor beside her, and starts speaking in Korean at an incredible rate. Every once in a while, Haeja interrupts her to tell me what is being said.

"*Aye, nae jook get da,* I'm dying, Haeja-ya," says Halmoni Kao-hai-dong. "I cannot sleep since I heard you were coming back home to visit your old grandmother. I keep everyone awake all night, smoking cigarettes, drinking coffee, even having a few shots of whiskey to make me calm down. I'm as nervous as a little child since I heard you were coming, Haeja-ya. Goddamn, goddamnit. . . ."

Grandma searches under the low table, behind the pillow she sits on.

"Where are those goddamn cigarettes?"

Hae-Soon points to the pocket sewn into her hanbok. Halmoni laughs and takes them out, then resumes her swearing and mumbling.

"Where is that goddamn lighter Lee Sa-bong brought back from his trip to Saudi Arabia?"

Hae-Soon smiles at me, nods knowingly at Haeja, and points to the other pocket. Grandma lights her cigarette, coughs, where was she, she asks, ah, yes, she answers, patting Haeja's knee with her gnarled hand.

"You know what happens to your old grandmother when she gets nervous, I have dreams about my father. The day before your arrival, the day you arrived, every night until you got here now, my father visits me in these dreams. Father, I tell him, I'm a busy old woman. Shit, I ain't got time to fuck around with anything, my granddaughter is coming to visit. Please, I tell him, Father, understand, you are my great ancestor ghost, but my old mind is playing tricks on me all night, I need my concentration to welcome Haeja back home. But then Lee Sa-bong said that maybe my father visits me in dreams just to let me know that I'm not going to die before I see Haeja and her daughter." Grandma stubs out her cigarette and chuckles to herself.

"Aigo, Haeja-ya, you were a mischievous girl. Do you re-member when you ran off to that radio station when you were nine years old and sang on that talent hour? Do you remember when you got lost in the mountains behind our little house near the zoo?" She doesn't give Haeja time to answer. "Did your sister tell you what a silly thing she did this morning? She went to Midopa department store and bought me a cosmetic case. Wanted me to wear some makeup to greet you." She laughs so hoarsely that she practically chokes. "The last time I wore makeup, I was a young girl. My husband went off to Seoul. My goddamn husband. My bald-headed father sent him from our home to study. Damn, damn. Goddamn. Sometimes I would like to find that husband of mine and tie his arms to one set of horses and his legs to another set of horses, and send the horses off at a gallop—rip him to pieces. . . ."

"Now, don't be silly," Hae-Soon says.

Kao-hai-dong Halmoni winks at me. "Tell Michael Sa-bong that I'm only teasing."

She laughs again and lights a cigarette. She asks one of the maids to bring her another cup of coffee, but Hae-Soon tells the maid that Grandma has had enough for the day.

"That's all I have," says Grandma Oh. "Coffee and ciga-rettes, my only friends." She stares out the window at the children playing in the little courtyard.

"My bald-headed father should have sent me to study in-stead of that husband of mine. I had brains. I should have said to my bald-headed father, Your honor, I'm a very bright, intel-ligent young woman, and I think you ought to send me instead of that husband of mine to one of those new schools opening up in Seoul for young women, the kind Lady Hwang went to. I bet that would have gotten his attention. I should have said, Your honor, the world is changing. Send your daughter Lon to

Seoul to take the degrees and be the scholar of the family. My father liked me a lot. Who knows, maybe he would have said yes."

As the two sisters and their grandmother continue to talk, Haeja translates more selectively. I will have to wait until later to find out all that is said.

Chul-Hee, the Lees' youngest child, puts on his sneakers and goes out to bounce a rubber ball in the courtyard. I go outside, put on my shoes, and join him. By now, I am like an old friend. Behind us, up the steps, I hear the women talking and laughing with animation. A pot of barley tea sits on a low table, the steam rising gently in the air.

Near the garden wall purple azaleas bloom. Here in the heart of Seoul, the air is filled with the scent of cherry and apple blossom. A light breeze lulls over the rooftops.

Chul-Hee goes off and returns with two shovels and a pail. He gestures for me to follow him to a sandbox in the corner, and together we dig sand. The shoveling brings back that fantasy: if I dig deep enough, will I come out backward in China again, or because I am in Korea, perhaps if I dig deep enough I'll discover America?

When I go back inside, Grandma Oh is in the midst of another tale.

"There's nothing wrong with a good woman marrying twice," she says.

Mrs. Han, of course, did marry twice, and I have often wondered how Grandma Oh reconciled her old-fashioned views on this matter with her daughter-in-law's decision. But as Haeja translates her remarks, I realize that Halmoni is referring to a television soap opera she follows. I wonder if she realizes how appropriate the storyline is to Mrs. Han.

Haeja has told me how, in the midst of World War II, Hal-

moni's son Dr. Oh married Song-Hee, the youngest daughter
of Dr. and Lady Hwang, my wife's maternal grandparents. The
day the atomic bomb was dropped on Hiroshima, Hae-Soon
was born. Two years later came Haeja. A few years after that,
on the day the Korean War started, June 25, 1950, Hae-Chul
was born.

Shortly after the birth of his son, Dr. Oh, already middle-
aged, volunteered to minister to the wounded and dying. Six
months later, he was missing in action. A few years later Halmoni was informed that her son had been captured, put on a
forced march, and died of frostbite in a North Korean prison.

"Tambae," she says, shaking out a Turtle Ship, a Korean filter
cigarette.

"Komsohapnida," I thank her, taking one from her pack.

For as long as anyone can remember, Kao-hai-dong Halmoni
has smoked a pack of strong cigarettes every day. She used to
smoke unfiltered cigarettes, but lately her cough has gotten so
bad that Mr. Lee has advised her to switch to Turtle Ships,
named for the first ironclads invented by Admiral Yi Sun-Sin.

Grandma Oh pats my knee and laughs. She has good *nunchi*
for my *kibun,* and I for hers. *Kibun* is a person's mood, his
unspoken aura, while *nunchi* is one's ability to read that mood
sensitively. If a man stays out all night drinking with his hostess girlfriend, even if he does not smell or act any different, his
wife's *nunchi* picks up that perfumeless aura about her husband, his foul *kibun,* as it were.

A long ash burns down to Grandma's little fingers, and at the
last moment she flicks the butt into an ashtray we have
brought her as a present. It is of clear glass molded in the shape
of a duck—the cigarette rests on the tail feathers—and the
object seems to delight her.

One of the old housemaids comes out of the kitchen door on

the other side of the courtyard, puts on her rubber shoes, and pads across and up the steps to us. Grandma rattles off some orders.

"Too early," Haeja exclaims.

"What?" I ask.

"She told the ajima to bring you some beer."

Mr. Lee comes back into the room. He says that for Halmoni and himself it is never too early to have a drink, and he gestures for the maid to bring back several *makju.* The maid bows and exits backward, steps into her rubber shoes, and scurries across the courtyard into the kitchen.

Grandma laughs again—a gritty, bluesy laugh—as she gestures for Haeja to calm down.

"Gain-cha-na," she says. "That's all right."

Several large brown bottles of OB beer arrive, and Halmoni pours out foamy glassfuls for me, Mr. Lee, and herself. It is not as cold as I like it, but cool enough to slake my thirst.

"Kom Bai," she toasts.

Mr. Lee and I toast, too, and he breaks out into a good-hearted, deep-bellied laugh. I have liked him from the moment we met at the airport. He is big and tough, probably even a little scary to some people, but I can see that he is a good man. I can also tell that he, too, is a great fan of Grandma Oh.

Grandma wants to know when I was born, Haeja says. I give her the date, but I don't know the hour. She shakes her head, and says something to Haeja, who tells me that I have to find out the exact time so that Halmoni can discover my fortune.

"Maye-kool. . . ."

As Halmoni pats my knee and says my name in her old accent, it strikes me that her memory of the world includes the last dynasty, when Korea was still an agrarian society, the fabled "hermit nation." I feel that if I can explicate the furrows,

68

the cracks, the wrinkles, the deep lines on her cheeks and her brow, in her chin and along the bridge of her nose, I would understand all there is to know about Korea.

Some of those wrinkles on Grandma Oh's face map the truce that was made between her late son's wife and herself. But it also involved a kind of treaty with Mr. Han. Grandma would raise her son's three children, and the Hans would raise Mr. Han's three children and the two children that the Hans had together. In the end, one of the Han children, Byung-Su, came to live with Grandma Oh as well.

As we get ready to leave and go back to Haeja's mother's house an old fishmonger appears in the middle of the courtyard with a tub of fish.

Grandma Oh shuffles over to the tub to examine the day's catch. This is one of the daily routines that have kept her busy and alive for so many years. She picks up one fish, throws it down, picks up another, examines it carefully.

"This fucking fish has bad eyes," she shouts at the fishmonger. "I won't buy from you if you keep bringing this shitty old fish. I'll have Hae-Soon call a fish market in Inchon and have it delivered fresh daily."

"But, Grandma-ya," the fishmonger says, "I got these croaker from Inchon this morning."

"That's all right, Halmoni," Hae-Soon says, stepping between them.

"Let's worry about the fish later," Mr. Lee says. "Michael and Haeja are going home."

Grandma picks through the tub of fish until she finds four or five acceptable ones, then hands them to one of the housemaids, arguing with the fishmonger even as she makes her purchase.

69

Haeja smiles at me. "Grandma never changes," she says in English. "In grade school, the other children showed up with their well-dressed mothers. We were accompanied by a funky little old lady, cigarette dangling from her mouth, laughing and hacking even back then."

One of the maids pays the fishmonger, who bows good-bye, smiling at Grandma Oh as if to say that both of them have played their parts well today. When the fishmonger is out of earshot, Grandma says, "Her fucking fish always have bad eyes. Next time we buy fish from the other fish lady." But her anger leaves as quickly as it came. She laughs, coughs again and again, then simply laughs as though Haeja and I were not there, and says to Hae-Soon, "Haeja is a mother and wife now, can you believe that? Hae-Soon-ah, I tell you, they have good kim-chee in Mi-Guk. These Americans are so tall."

She turns to pull on Haeja's arm. "I'm going to visit you one day in Mi-Guk. You take me up to the top of the Empire State Building and we'll go see the Niagara Falls, who knows, maybe even the Grand Canyon. Maybe one day when my work is finished around here and Hae-Soon's children are older . . ." She pauses. "But who would take care of the old ajima if I was gone?" Then she says, "Yet maybe soon I'll hop on one of those planes at Kimpo and go visit you in New York. I'll bet there's a grandpa there who would really find me goddamn attractive and interesting, don't you think? Don't you think, Haeja-ya? There is probably a nice old grandpa in New York who would really like Kao-hai-dong Halmoni. . . ."

"Time to take a nap," Hae-Soon sings.

Grandma goes back up the big steps, waving good-bye to us.

"You know I'm getting old when Haeja is a mother and wife, don't you?" Then she adds, "There's nothing wrong with a good woman marrying twice. Nothing at all. This is a new era."

MORNING CALM

삼
청
공
원

The only people awake are some of the ajima and a houseboy cleaning the floor. One of the ajima is brewing a big pot of barley tea, and I nod good morning to her. She hands me a cup and I go to the low table. Another ajima, who has constant problems with her teeth and her husband, comes in the back door with a bowl of soy paste. The Han family members are still asleep in the various bedrooms of the house.

After I drink the tea, I take my running shoes off a shelf by the back door (shoes are not worn in a Korean house), put them on, and go out into the yard to stretch. Mr. Yun, the foreman, and some of his men who are building a new house for Mr. Han are already at work. I say good morning to Yun and nod hello to the workmen.

On the other side of the house I hear the squish-squish of rubber shoes, a maid venturing out for a bowl of kochoo-

chang, the red pepper paste, and kim-chee from the giant urns
out behind the kitchen. One afternoon, when I played hide-
and-seek with my daughter, she gave me a scare by disappearing behind the urns, as suddenly as if a ghost had kidnapped
her into the air.

I run down the hill to Samchung-dong. Though the sun has
not come up over the mountain, the street is already alive with
old and young people, going to exercise in the park.

Bicycle wheels creak. Silk coats rustle; silk pants woosh back
and forth. A car engine stirs. The clappers of the Buddhist
temple announce that yet another morning has begun. A po-
liceman stands at the intersection of Samchung-dong and the
road that leads to Hae-Soon's house. Students in military
fatigues stand in front of a tea house, sipping themselves
awake. Soldiers wait around talking on the corner. The tiny
shops on Samchung-dong open their doors. A woman sweeps
the sidewalk in front of her candy store, and a boy sweeps in
front of his parents' noodle shop; across the street, an old man
hoses down the pavement around his vegetable stall. A low
hum invades Seoul. The air slowly fills with commerce—car
and bus exhausts—and of tradition—the aroma of kim-chee,
garlic, onions. Though already crowded, the street is free of
litter.

I cross the street to where sidewalk and paved lanes give way
to the dirt road leading into the park. The cars move by quickly
and closely, so I pay attention to where I'm going.

"*Anyong-hasaeyo*," an old man bows hello.

"*Anyong*," I say, nodding.

A young tough barrels into me, does not say "*Mianhamnida*,"
Excuse me, and crashes on down the roadway.

The yellow-brown granite mountains around Samchung
Park are tinged with the greens of juniper, pine, oak, and elm,

and covered by a purple wash as the sun rises through the
city's haze. Seoul is granite and concrete; here in the park there
are dirt paths, though there are cement gutters to funnel the
spillover from the streams down to drainpipes near the park's
entrances. Because of the tall trees, there is an abundance of
oxygen in the air, and none of the polluted smell of the city
below. There are no tall buildings in this district, only homes
and two- and three-story shops. Overhead a hawk glides on
the currents of the morning air.

High school boys are playing volleyball before class or bat-
ting a shuttlecock without a net in a rapid-fire badminton
volley. Older boys do tai-chi or taikwondo. They shadowbox,
spar with open hands, dancing over the stones. Morning in
Seoul does not come gradually; it tends to explode at first light.

The dirt path I run on has been pounded hard and flat, and
slopes steeply upward. Running nearly vertically, thighs sore,
calves stiff, I just manage to read the Korean syllables on the
sign pinned to the green cyclone fence—BEWARE—when I come
on two soldiers. I run in place for a few seconds, not breaking
my stride, before I turn and go back down the trail. Some
places are off-limits: the highest points in the city, the top of
this mountain, the mountain next to it that leads up to the wall
of the ancient city.

BOOM!

The granite earth trembles from the concussion.

Dynamite, I think. I heard it the first morning, inside the
mountain, near the tunnel that leads into the northern part of
Seoul.

Oh Haeja's anxious face looms before me. My wife worries
that wandering off by myself, I am going to get lost. She has
a schoolgirl notion that North Korean guerrillas infiltrate the
city at night, hiding in the mountains and in the parks, espe-

cially in the northern part of the city. As an American, I will be an easy target for these commandos, she fears.

There is a lot about Korea that I don't understand and that scares me, like the explosion, which I hear nearly every day, but being killed by commandos as I run in the park is not one of my fears. Still, I turn and cut back down the saddle of the hill, built rock on rock, boulder on boulder, along the pathway, the way this whole republic is built. ROK, a perfect acronym for this mountainous, craggy, granite land.

At the park gate I stop, fatigued from the ascent and the mountain air.

I order a Lotte soda at a small stand in the park and sit down at one of the tables. The early light filters down through its bleached-out canvas awning, amber and smoky. I think of having a cigarette; I wish I had a notebook to write in.

Children play in the small open area in front of me, on the seesaw and swings, the jungle gym and monkey bars. A few high school girls gossip at a nearby table. Old men sit chatting with each other on a bench. One of them saunters over and sits down without asking my permission. He asks if I am an American. Unlike the other old men in the park, who wear traditional baggy pants with rubber shoes, billowing white jackets, and an occasional ancient horsehair hat, he wears dark slacks, Western-style leather shoes, and wire-rim glasses, and has on a neatly pressed white short-sleeved polyester shirt with four patch pockets, sort of like the guayabera shirts that Spanish men wear in my old neighborhood in New York. He is spryer than the other men, perhaps even a bit younger. He offers me a Turtle Ship cigarette, which I accept, then lights his and mine with a Zippo. There is a familiarity to his gestures, as though we have known each other a long time and have sat at this open-air café often.

"Korea was a country long before Jesus was born," he says in heavily accented English, blowing out smoke. Still, he speaks quite well. Some men of his generation read Chinese and many know a little Japanese, but few speak or understand English.

He sees that he has my attention, and like an old actor, he takes his time now. He waves his arms around: "Mountains," he says, "everywhere you look there are mountains. You forget that the Han River flows to the sea, that Korea is surrounded by thousands of tiny islands." He takes out a sheet of paper and a tiny pencil and draws two Chinese characters. "Look," he says. *"Ban-do,* Chinese word, it means half island."

But I don't get it.

"Peninsula," he says, "the Sino-Korean words for peninsula." He points to the first character. "This is the character for a cow being cut in half," he informs me, and I nod dumbly. He goes to the next character. "Bird resting on mountain," he says. I nod as though I understand, but I don't. With his right hand, he places the tip of his thumb behind the first joint of his index finger, a gesture in Korea for a very small measure or portion.

"Maybe you understand this much?" he asks.

"Maybe not even that much," I confess.

"Ah," he says, laughing. "You do not understand Chinese characters, only *Hangul.*"

"Not even the Korean alphabet," I say. "But at least I'm working on that."

"How long you study?"

"Five years," I answer.

He laughs.

"King Sejong said a wise man can acquaint himself with the alphabet before the morning is over."

"Well," I respond, "it's taken me a lot longer than that."

75

"A stupid man, he said, can learn them in ten days." Perhaps it's time to go home for breakfast. Sensing my displeasure, the old man gestures for me to wait: "The king was speaking about Koreans," he tells me. "Foreigners would naturally take longer to learn the alphabet. And it is a beautiful alphabet. Think of this. You can make the sound of the wind in Korean, the cry of a crane, the cackle of fowl, and the barking of dogs. All these sounds may be written in Hangul. But I was telling you about the word 'peninsula.' You see, when General MacArthur planned his famous amphibious invasion at Inchon Harbor near the outset of the Korean War, he was not concerned that the peninsula was a half island. He was concerned with cutting the peninsula in half. Inchon, with one of the highest tides in the world, gave him his entrée. From there, MacArthur drove a wedge through the half island. What got him in trouble with President Truman was deploying the troops northward to the Yalu, where he planned to use nuclear weapons. This is why many Koreans do not like Harry Truman, not because he did not let the general use nuclear weapons—we are all grateful for that—but because he knew nothing about Korea, and so hordes of Chinese soldiers entered the war, pushing the Americans and South Koreans hundreds of miles to the south, just above the city of Taegu."

"That is where my wife is from," I say. "She wasn't even three years old then."

"Now do you see the importance of understanding history?" he asks—but I'm not sure of the connection he's trying to make.

"If the Communists had gone farther south, you would not be exercising in Samchung Park this morning." He stands suddenly and goes to the concession stand, where he orders two coffees. I want to say that I don't know him and need to get back, but he must sense that.

"My name is Dr. Kim," he says. "And yours?"

As I tell him the thought crosses my mind that the old man is compiling a dossier on me.

"Interesting," he responds. "Two last names, two first names, last name and first name either way a first or last name."

"Not quite," I tell him. "Not too many people have the first name Stephens."

"True, true," he answers. "You have the same last name as the poet."

"Wallace Stevens spells his name with a *v,*" I say.

"I mean James Stephens, the Irish poet, the author of *The Crock of Gold.*"

Dr. Kim asks if I studied much about Korea before coming here, and I tell him that I have tried to read as much as possible, that lately I am even reading various Chinese works that I had heard influenced Korean thought—Confucius, of course, but also Mencius, *The Great Learning, I Ching* and, "of course," I say, "Lao-tzu has always been my favorite author."

"Hmmm, curious," he says, "this notion of a 'favorite' author—a very American habit, yes?" Then thinking that through further, he says, "I guess *my* 'favorite' Korean author is Yi Hwang. Do you know his work?"

I don't.

"Rather than singular beings, Yi saw the essential interlocking and mutually dependent relationships of everyone, even everything. Already during your stay in Seoul you must have seen how Koreans always work together. Our households don't have one maid but many, each helping the other, helping the mother, who is helping her husband and children. We have none of your rugged individualists as in America—no Paul Bunyans, no Huckleberry Finns. We are a nation of rugged people working together.

"Yi wrote about the fear of death, too. Whereas some might stop their studies and work when someone close to them died, Yi said that Chu Hsi worked harder. Why? Because learning is the greatest joy in life. Elsewhere he said that the body was merely the result of others nurturing and developing it, whereas the mind is uniquely our own. We are not a bunch of automatons following a leader mindlessly. In fact, we are a nation of thinkers, and you can't have thinkers unless people learn to use their minds well and fully. But unlike your ideas in the west of ids and egos, libidos and superegos, right- and left-lobe thinking, we think of a person having two minds, the constant and the changeable. All this is from Yi Hwang, so I think you understand why he is my *favorite* writer.

"The constant mind works in the past, present, and future. The changeable mind is more sense-oriented, being like a desire for a cigarette, a cup of tea, a drink of alcohol, or making love to a beautiful woman. We Koreans share a constant mind. With a constant mind, fear of death is overcome. The changeable mind is at the mercy of the senses. A constant mind feels the pains and comforts of others as though they were his or her own."

I say nothing, listening attentively, enjoying the strength of another Turtle Ship, feeling good inside about my run, but equally good about this cigarette now, sitting at the café, watching the sun rise over the park and, down below, over the city. In many respects, the old man and the setting and the hour fit perfectly into some kind of preconceived notion I had about Korea. The modern city is a mile or so away. Here much is perhaps as it had been a long time ago. Kerouac's *Dharma Bums,* taekwando artists, Korea's *hwarang,* the noble poetic warriors of ancient Silla. All of these details crowd my head as the old man smokes and talks. His openness reminds me of Grandma Oh, and I begin to see that longevity itself is a great virtue.

"You must find some of his writings in translation," he says. "Try the Royal Asiatic Society Bookshop, that is a good place for Korean books in English."

Maybe because he is old and simply passing his time, he rambles.

"You have read about the Three Kingdoms?"

"A little—"

"You see," he says, "there were various clans and factions, but finally the nation formed into three kingdoms." Silla, Koguryo, and Paekche, active and independent of China, I think, regarding his three kingdoms. I may know only a few phrases, but I've read my history books, I want to say but keep quiet. The truth is that I know very little. He tells me how Silla unified the country in the seventh century and speaks of the Koryo dynasty from the tenth through the fourteenth centuries. He asks if I have read anything by the great Koryo Buddhist poet T'aego, and I say that I have not.

"T'aego said that we must study until we know nothing," adds Dr. Kim.

Then his mind seems to drift away from these heady topics. He sips his coffee and lights another cigarette, staring off at the children playing.

"Red ginseng is better than the white," he says. "You try ginseng root. You will run better." I look around at the other old men, marveling at their longevity, and the antiquity of their manners and dress. But Dr. Kim is not quite that old yet;

his hair is only slightly gray, and his sinewy arms suggest that he still has a lot of strength.

"I am a doctor," he says. "Oh, I should say I *was* a doctor. In America. But now I'm retired, so I came home to Seoul." He stubs out his cigarette and stares out at the playing field.

"I was born the year the Japanese officially annexed Korea," he says.

"1910."

"Yes," he says, "1910. A very bad time for everything Korean." He pauses, seeming to lose his breath, then goes on. "You should learn as much as you can about Korea, so that when you go back home, you can tell everyone what the country really was like and is now."

I thank him and stand to go.

"Wait!"

I stop.

"My grandson," says Dr. Kim, "he lives in California, goes to MIT in Cambridge, he is visiting me for the summer. Maybe you have seen him in the park. Like yourself, he is a jogger. Have you seen him in the park?"

I say that I haven't.

"Now I'm going to get in trouble with my wife," I tell him. "She worries when I stay out for too long."

"Have you visited Kyung-Bok Palace?"

"Many times," I say.

"Have you visited the pavilion behind the throne room where the scribes worked on the Korean language?"

I haven't.

"You must go there," he says, shaking his finger at me. "It is right behind the throne room."

"Not today," I say. "But maybe tomorrow."

80

"As soon as possible," he says.

I get up to leave.

He calls after me that if I run into his grandson, I should say hello, tell him I know his grandfather.

"Did you go to Harvard?" he calls.

"No, no," I laugh.

"Where, then?"

I don't answer him.

"Where did you go to school?" he calls again.

This seems to be a terribly important question for him and for many Koreans—here, you need to attend the right schools to get anywhere in life. It used to be that if you attended Kyongi High School and Seoul National University, you were set for life. This was the equivalent of Britain's Oxbridge connection and America's old-boy network.

"My family is waiting for me," I say, leaving. "They'll be worried if I don't get back soon."

"Visit the Scribe Pavilion."

"I will," I say.

As I walk away from the old man and out of the park I hear him singing in a deep, resonant voice. Confucius loved music; so did King Sejong. The Mongolian conquerors were said to love music, too, and introduced the large orchestras into the Yi palace.

When I turn around one last time, I see the old man in the distance, waving. I wave back. I can't see him any more, but as he turns to walk away, I still hear him singing what sounds like "Arirang," the unofficial Korean national anthem. But I might be wrong. Maybe it is the aria from some Western opera. Maybe it is just a pop song he heard on the radio that morning, or an old folk song he learned as a boy. I think: Music must come easily to a people with a language that can replicate the sound of the wind, the calling of the crane, the cackle of fowl, and the barking of a dog, not to mention the sounds of a cane tapping the cobbles at first light, the crow of a rooster, the flight of sparrows, the yatter of the magpie, the hiss of a cat, even the sound of morning calm.

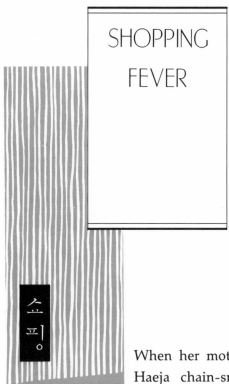

SHOPPING
FEVER

When her mother is not in the house, Haeja chain-smokes cigarettes in the bathroom. If I have a drink, she takes it from me, slugs down the whiskey or beer willfully, grinding her teeth, gritting her jaw.

Nearly every morning I hear Mrs. Han discussing the word *mut-sheet-da,* "taste," with her visiting daughter.

"Op-da," Mrs. Han says, "It does not exist."

"Is-so-yo," Haeja says, "Yes, it does exist."

Taste in food, cigarettes, drinks, clothes, shoes, hairdos, life-styles, generations, countries, families, cars, earrings, furniture, paintings, voice registers, musicianship. Can two women who are so alike have tastes more different than do Haeja and her mother?

Because I am an American, my haphazard dress, which an actor friend once described as sloppy Ivy League, has so far gone unmolested, although Mrs. Han keeps offering to buy me some suits, and Haeja keeps vetoing her. But now, with a formal dinner party at the house imminent, Mrs. Han has the upper hand regarding the matter.

"What does Michael want?" her mother asks.

"Nothing," her daughter answers.

"Nothing?"

"That's right," says Haeja, "he doesn't need anything. He doesn't want anything. We live very simply back in America."

"Suits," her mother says.

"Suits?"

"He needs many suits," Mrs. Han insists.

"Mother," Haeja says, "he doesn't wear suits."

"Why?"

"He's not a businessman, he doesn't work in the government."

"For the university," her mother parries.

"They dress casually at American universities," the daughter says.

"Too casual," responds mother, shaking her head.

"Just casual enough."

But I do need something other than my wrinkly olive green linen suit for the dinner party, so Mrs. Han strikes the first compromise by buying for me a store-bought, off-the-rack suit in Myong-dong, the shopping district.

Here in Korea, Haeja must assume traditional roles that require her piety to heaven above, to her parents on earth, to her siblings in general. She must also be my wife, not in the sense that we have defined it over five years of marriage, but as it has been defined over a few millennia by Confucius and his followers. And sometimes she bristles at this duty.

It was Confucius who said that women and servants are hard to deal with: if you are familiar with them, they stop being humble, if you remain distant, they resent you.

Ten years ago, when Haeja first came to America, she was a young rebel, smoking, drinking, wearing heavy makeup, dressing western-style in denim skirts and peasant blouses from secondhand shops on the Lower East Side. Within moments of arriving back in Korea her universe has altered drastically; affection for her siblings and righteousness toward her parents is expected, but she must also be aware of the separate functions of a husband and a wife and must reacquaint herself with the rules governing how to address the young and elderly. Above all, she must not go too far: she must know her own place, not as she defined it as a musician in New York City, but as a daughter and sister in Seoul.

Her duties and responsibilities to her stepfather are easy enough to manage. The relationship is cordial, even undemanding, and open. What constantly gets to Haeja is her mother, and if I were to ask her mother what gets under her skin, the answer would probably be her daughter Haeja. It seems to me that the Han household would not exist if it were not for Mrs. Han's unflagging desire to hold it together, to educate her children, to find them spouses, to buy them homes, to set them up in business, if necessary. Even her eccentricities fascinate me: her faith in fortune-tellers, her folk theories about illness and health, her weakness for health fads (the current one is drinking lemon juice at every meal), her constant kibitzing, and her continual insistence on doing everything her way. But these same qualities seem to annoy Haeja to the core.

Perhaps the differences between them have to do with upbringing. Mrs. Han was the fourth and youngest daughter of a doctor-poet. Her mother was one of the first Korean women to be formally educated and a shrewd business person, amassing a fortune from her apple orchards in Taegu. Mrs. Han's life was privileged, compared to those of other children. In the Korean provinces during the Japanese occupation, there was nothing like the incredible acquisitions of wealth found in Seoul today. Lady Hwang was a well-known disciplinarian, but she was uncharacteristically soft on Song-Hee, her youngest, who was frail. Mrs. Han was her father's pet as well, and even today, her middle-aged sisters rib her about how spoiled she was.

But Haeja scarcely lived with her mother. Instead, she was raised by Grandma Oh, her father's mother, while her mother embarked on a new life with Mr. Han. After the Korean War, the family moved from Taegu to Seoul, where Mrs. Han set up various businesses with one of her sisters, also a widow—beauty parlors for American officers' wives and mistresses, a seaweed export business, a dry cleaning service.

Since yesterday the house has been bustling with ajima, chefs, and temporary help. The formal dining room has been opened, and the table, which easily seats fifteen, has been set with placemats and linen and crystal glasses, china and silverware, chopsticks and spoons. Various condiments are already set out, *paek* and other milder kim-chees, sesame leaves, sugared seaweed, and plates of cucumber flavored with soy sauce, sugar, onion, garlic, sesame oil, red pepper threads, and sesame seed. To stay out of the way, I sit in the dining room, drinking a cup of coffee and reading the *Korea Times.*

The dinner is to be a traditional Korean meal, but seasoned to Western tastes—that is, less spicy. In the kitchen the chef is tyrannizing the staff. But many of the ajima have been in the household so long that they have assumed Mrs. Han's nervous system as their own: when she is up, they are up, and when she is down, they are down. Now, because she is nervous, they are nervous, and everyone is constantly yelling at each other, then immediately apologizing.

The young houseman comes into the living room with a tray of soft drinks, trips on the edge of a rug, and sends glasses, ice, and bottles shattering across the floor. Several ajima quickly clean up the mess, but not without cursing him. Everyone has told Mrs. Han to get rid of the houseman because he's a numb-skull, but perversely she has taken him under her wing, practically adopting him. He is a born-again Christian who goes into ecstatic trances in his little room out behind the house. A vegetarian, he eschews the communal meal with the other household workers. Mrs. Han is trying to help him get a visa to live with his sister in Ohio.

The guests at dinner include a European couple who are the Hans' best friends; he is a businessman and president of the Royal Asiatic Society. There are also an American embassy couple, the wife involved with Korean folk art and pottery; the Canadian ambassador and his wife; the Spanish ambassador, and two Korean couples. The meal begins with a light broth, followed by three kinds of fish and two kinds of meat—*bulgoki,* barbecued beef, and *kalbi,* short ribs. There are also traditional root dishes: *kosari,* which is an earthy color and has the texture of cooked string beans, and snow-colored *doragi,* which is chewy like glutinous rice.

Mr. Han sits quietly at the head of the table, neither uncomfortable nor fully at ease. Mrs. Han, at her end, fairly bubbles over, recommending one fish dish, passing vegetables, telling one of her guests about the chekkori, a rare horizontal book painting that covers nearly the entire north wall.

"Ceremonial wooden ducks used to be so easy to find," says the American woman, seated on my right.

"Yes," I nod, uncertainly.

"They were so affordable when we first came to Korea," she continues, "but a few years ago, David Rockefeller came through town and bought up all the wooden ducks he could find, and once he left, the prices escalated."

"Is she telling you about the fate of wooden ducks?" her husband asks.

He is a well-scrubbed, nearly squeaky-clean midlevel embassy official, his gray suit Brooks Brothers, his shirt button-down, his tie rep, the shoes he left at the door big clunky brogans. His teeth are horsey and spotlessly white, his smile boyishly ingratiating. He's built like an athlete, maybe a college baseball player turned amateur tennis buff. He tells me that he's read some of my writing, which startles me, since I don't recall telling anyone that I'm a writer. He notices my surprise and tells me that Mrs. Han showed him my book about Tangun.

At the end of the table, the antique Spanish ambassador looks as though he has just wandered off the set of a sequel to Buñuel's *Discreet Charm of the Bourgeoisie*.

"I am too old for diplomacy," he says. "Too old for parties. In a week, I return home to my Madrid."

"Señor Rodriquez was the first ambassador from Spain after the war," Mr. Han informs me.

"Have some more food," Mrs. Han prods the old Spaniard.

"Too spicy," he says.

"But Mrs. Han especially made the food mild for her Western guests," the American woman says.

"I am an old man," the Spanish ambassador confesses. "Sometimes barley tea tastes too spicy."

"Mr. Ambassador once taught everyone in Seoul how to do the flamenco dance," Mrs. Han tells me.

"Ah, flamenco," the old man sighs.

Through the centerpiece of wildflowers I spot the Canadian ambassador, talking economics with one of the Korean guests as though the subject were as fascinating as sex.

At the beginning of the meal, the oldest ajima has what amounts to a nervous breakdown—she can't get it straight to which side of each guest she is supposed to serve from. She is quickly replaced by one of the chef's staff, a man obviously familiar with dinners like this. Some of the young temporary maids have giggle-fits, and they too are replaced by other male assistants to the chef. From there, it's smooth sailing, food and talk and drink, and then more talk with coffee, whereupon we all adjourn to the living room for dessert and drinks.

"Those damn Indians," I hear the Canadian ambassador say. "They have oil on their reservations, but won't let the government lease the land." Then to me: "Have you been following this debate about human rights?"

I nod yes.

"You Americans need the Republicans in power," he says. Hmmmm, I say.

"Ask the Koreans," he says, "if you don't believe me."

"Darling," the American woman says to her husband, "did you see this wonderful Chinese medicine chest?" She's drawn to it, no doubt, by the large wooden ceremonial duck sitting on top of it. I imagine her thinking: Who knows what you'd pay for something like this?

The Spanish ambassador sits down with a glass of cognac.

"Spanish?" he asks.

"Irish," Haeja says, answering for me. "Black Irish."

The old man strains to looks at Haeja; he squints and focuses, then looks perplexed. "You don't look Irish," he says to Haeja.

"Him," she says, pointing to me.

"But he's Spanish," he says. "Like myself. Are you not Spanish, too?"

Haeja says. "I'm Mrs. Han's daughter. We live in America. In New York City."

"Ah, Mrs. Han," the old ambassador sighs.

"To Mrs. Han," the American embassy employee says, raising his cognac.

"Ten thousand years!" his wife shouts.

"Hear! Hear!" the Canadian ambassador says, raising his glass.

The Spanish ambassador looks confused, and the Canadian leans over to remind him that this is the Han residence.

"Well, then," the old man says, "perhaps it is time for siesta." He gets up to leave. I walk with Mrs. Han to the formal entrance of the house, where I search through the pile for the old man's shoes.

"The Hwang family has beautiful daughters," the old man tells Mrs. Han, giving her pecks on both cheeks.

"You mean the Han family," Mrs. Han corrects him.

"Oh, the Han family is all right," the ambassador says. "I am talking about you and your sisters, and that lovely mother of yours. How is she?"

"She died," Mrs. Han says. She does not add that that was twenty years ago.

"I'm sorry to hear that," the ambassador replies. "I remember that she was such a good dancer. What a shame. I'll miss her when I retire."

The Canadian ambassador and his wife excuse themselves next, leaving the American and Korean couples and the Hans' friends from Belgium. The American woman has been working on a big glass of cognac and is now quite drunk.

"Wonderful," she says.

"What?" one of the Koreans asks.

"She's wonderful," the American woman says.

"Who?"

"Mrs. Han, of course. Have you seen her mother and sisters? The whole family," she says. "They make Korea seem like a matriarchy." Mrs. Han is tall and thin, Haeja small and broad-shouldered, yet there is an unmistakable kinship in their faces—the bones, the lips, the eyes, and especially in the high-strung temperaments. Maybe their disagreements have to do with the fact that they are so much alike, and perhaps the tipsy American woman wasn't so far off in suggesting a matriarchal lineage.

Like her own mother, Mrs. Han is a successful business-woman. She sells the homes that her husband designs and builds, collects and sells folk paintings, and owns quite a bit of property in and around Seoul. Socially, she is something of a grande dame, like her mother, too—a born diplomat, almost a butterfly among embassy wives and cultural figures. But no matter how liberated her manner at times, she is very much of her generation: she fully subscribes to the Confucian ordering of the world. Of course, she breaches that belief daily as de facto head of the household, and in her business dealings, but in those respects she really is no different from hundreds of other well-off wives married to important men in Seoul. In fact, I have heard it said that the yangban men of the Yi dynasty also disdained daily practical matters as well and left them to their wives. Noblemen thought, spoke, wrote, philosophized, posed; noblewomen handled the household nuts and bolts.

But there are more layers to Mrs. Han's character than the traditional virtues, so many that at times her ambitions seems unfathomable. One of them, I know, is to be seen as the essence of propriety. In the social world she exudes refinement and tradition; privately she is the angel in the house who worries about keeping peace among three distinct families under one roof.

Among these families, Hae-Chul, the first son, has the most highly esteemed position in the Confucian world. Hailed as a prodigy, he has gone to the best schools, and had the attention of what has amounted to an absolute matriarchy—mother, sisters, grandmother, aunts, female cousins. Hae-Soon, Mrs. Han's oldest child, serves as her mother's amanuensis, her factotum. If Mrs. Han has dreams of diplomatic triumphs, inside and outside the household, it is Hae-Soon who implements all of her goodwill. Only Grandma Oh is more widely liked and respected.

Then there is Haeja, the middle child of Mrs. Han's oldest family. In appearance, I am told, Haeja is the very reincarnation of her father, Dr. Oh, Mrs. Han's first husband. And the missing father has made his presence felt in other realms of Haeja's life as well: other children treated her as a less-than, the logic being that you must have done something wrong that the Will of Heaven should have looked so poorly upon your fate. Any lingering innuendo was further fueled when the school principal singled her out of a file of children lined up in the schoolyard to give her an award for her late father's heroism during the war, and her own state of orphanhood.

Husbandless, Mrs. Han was expected, even so late as the

mid-twentieth century, to make the choice handed down to widows from the earliest days of the Yi dynasty: she could become a *kabu,* a woman who lives alone after her husband's death, or *yollyo,* a woman who drowns or hangs herself after her husband's death. Remarriage had been out of the question since the benign, egalitarian days of the Koryo dynasty a thousand years ago.

Influenced perhaps by the extraordinary circumstances in Korea after the war, Grandma Oh—herself a kabu—was quite open-minded about her daughter-in-law's liaison with Mr. Han, as was Mrs. Han's own mother, Lady Hwang. But some of her own sisters did not approve of their baby sister's behavior, and her worst critics were Mr. Han's relatives, especially one of his sisters. So perhaps her shrewdness grew from the habit of camouflaging herself against her detractors.

"What does Michael want?" her mother asks.

"Nothing," her daughter answers.

"Suits," her mother says.

"We've been through this a thousand times since I arrived."

"He needs more than one suit off a department store rack," Mrs. Han observes.

"Mother," Haeja says, "how many times do I have to tell you this: He doesn't wear suits."

"Why?" asks mother, as if for the first time.

"He's not a businessman, he doesn't work in the government," Haeja says, like an actress repeating her lines well.

"For the university," her mother offers, as if the thought had only just come into her head.

"I told you how people dress at American universities," the daughter says.

"Too casual," responds mother, shaking her head, her pronouncement like a judge in a court of law passing her final sentence.

"Just casual enough," the daughter says.

"Several suits," pleads Mrs. Han. "It takes five years to meet son-in-law, let your mother buy him some suits."

"But he doesn't wear suits."

"No matter," says Mrs. Han, nodding.

"Really," Haeja says.

"What does he want?"

"He doesn't need a suit."

"Several suits."

"He's not a businessman, he doesn't wear suits."

"In this country," her mother says, speaking as though *this country* is her household, "here in Seoul, he needs some good suits to get around. More guests are coming to dinner this week. We like to eat at hotels downtown. Father wants to take Michael to the nightclub at Walker Hill."

The old Mercedes glides down toward the center of Seoul. Mrs. Han has "shopping fever," and has decided to take me along.

At the light at the corner of Sejong-ro I look out at Kwanghwamun, the elaborate gate to the old city. If Seoul still has a center, this is it—two stories of pagoda-style roofs that seem to float in the air, defying gravity and the rules of architecture, guarded by giant turtle-bodied stone effigies, amid the modernity of the cultural center, the French and American embassies, and various hotels and newspaper offices.

Ornamental beasts hang over the edges of the rooftops, first among them is Sonogong, a monkey wearing a monk's hat.

Various legends attend this figure, who sets out in search of wisdom and eventually becomes a divine sage. Sonogong is able to turn himself into many different shapes and sizes; he is athletic and acrobatic, and is even thought by some to be immortal. In Seoul his presence on a building ensures success and health. He is a folk healer, too, and a guardian against foreign influences and invasions. I make sure to greet him warmly every time I pass the great old gate, to let him know that I come with the best of intentions.

Mother taps me on the shoulder. "You must be careful of your liver," she says, placing her hand over her own liver, patting it.

"My liver is fine," I answer.

"My fortune-teller tells me that you drink too much," she says.

"I'm Irish," I say. "You have kim-chee, the Irish have alcohol. It's unpatriotic not to drink, it's the only thing that my family and I have in common. They'd consider me a traitor if I didn't indulge."

"My father was a doctor, but he also wrote poetry," Mother goes on. "He had too many girlfriends, too. That and the alcohol killed him. He was only in his early forties. Writers must be careful of drinking too much and having too many girlfriends."

I think of asking how many girlfriends are too many, but then think better of it, not wanting to jeopardize the combination of openness and secretiveness, propriety and coyness she shows me. When we are alone together, Mrs. Han likes to tell me about her poet father, the doctor with too many girlfriends. She almost never speaks of her late mother, though everyone else in the family does.

.   .   .

"You saw the movie *The Godfather*?" Mr. Han had asked me.
"Yes," I'd answered, "many times."
"That is Grandma Hwang," he'd said, laughing. "The Mar-
lon Brando character."

"Today we get you fitted for a suit," Mrs. Han informs me
as the light changes and the car turns onto Sejong-ro.

We drive past the embassies, hotels, newspaper offices, and
the Sejong Cultural Center; past the big statue of Admiral Yi
Sun-Sin and the bell pagoda near Chongno. Minutes later we
are in front of the Seoul Plaza Hotel at the center of the city.
Across the street are Duk-Soo Palace and the old City Hall,
built by the Japanese. In front of the hotel, there is a great plaza
where five or six main arteries converge, and traffic comes to
a standstill.

Shopping makes Mrs. Han philosophical. "Marriage is like
the life of Yono and Seo," she intones. "Even if the man is the
sun, the wife is still the moon. Husband Yono wanders down
to the rocks to gather seaweed when suddenly a giant fish
carries him off to Japan, where he is considered so extraordinary that he is made king. When he does not return from his
fishing, wife Seo goes down to the rocks to see what happened
to her husband. There she finds his shoes. Yet, no sooner has
she discovered his shoes than she herself is carried off, not by
a giant fish but by the rock. She winds up in Japan, too. The
moment Seo leaves, the sun and moon disappear from the
heavens. Astrologers determine that the light has flown off to
Japan. Envoys travel abroad and are told by Yono that it is the
Will of Heaven that he should be Japan's king. He is sorry, but
he cannot leave. Instead, he gives the envoys a bolt of silk cloth
woven by Seo, instructing them to take it home and offer it as

a sacrifice to Heaven. Which is when the sun and moon return."

I don't understand any of this. But by now we have arrived and doormen are opening the car doors, greeting us. One symptom of shopping fever is apparently indiscriminate over-tipping, and Mrs. Han freely hands around the won.

We descend into what looks like a subway entrance, but turns out to be an entrance to the Bando Arcade, one of many flashy underground shopping malls in the downtown area.

Tailors, dressmakers, tie shops, record stores, jewelers, antique and art galleries, and tourist shops line both sides of the long, bright, shiny corridor, and shop owners stand in their doorways. Saying hello to Mrs. Han, they see the fever in her eyes.

Mrs. Han stops at an antique shop, and I linger outside, mulling over the story of Yono and Seo. The parity of Yono and Seo is almost unheard of in everyday Korea. Here, husband and wife are sun and moon, symbiosis. Woman controls the seas, man the fields. The sun and moon don't leave the sky until both man and woman have flown to Japan. Together, they are responsible for providing light to the heavens. The king regards them both so highly that he sends envoys to retrieve the couple. Though women don't dominate Korean folklore, they play essentially equal roles with men in those tales in which they do appear.

I'm reminded of yet another tale concerning a woman in an old Korean chronicle known as *The Nine-Cloud Dream*. A beautiful maiden falls in love with Shao Yu, the son of an immortal hermit. Determined to get Shao, the woman says: "Woman, all her life through, follows her husband. Happiness, unhappiness, failure, success depend on him. Me, I am not married yet, and even though I don't feel like being my own matchmaker, there is an old saying that can't be denied. The wise choose their own king." I take that to mean that the wiser a woman is, the more choices are available to her.

The story of Ch'unhyang is a fine example of a Korean folktale about a good woman who suffers. Entitled "The Song of a Faithful Wife," but generally referred to as Ch'unhyang, it chronicles the life of a daughter of Minister Song and a kisaeng, a female entertainer, who falls in love with Yi, the eldest son of a famous family in Seoul. Though he loves her, he goes back to the capital, promising to return. When her lover goes off, Ch'unhyang is forced to become a kisaeng, but she manages to defend her virtue and honor at all cost, even jail and the risk of death. A new governor comes to the province, and hearing about her beauty, he summons her and demands her hand in marriage immediately. She tells him that she cannot have two husbands, but the governor laughs at her virtuousness, saying that she was a mere diversion to Minister Yi from Seoul. But Ch'unhyang persists in her refusal, saying, "A subject cannot serve two kings and a wife cannot belong to two husbands." For this he sentences her to death, but eventually her lover returns to save her. Virtue, filial piety, the role of the illegitimate, the struggle of women, the will to be steadfast in the face of adversity, nearly all the major themes of Korean literature are found in this humble *p'ansori,* a so-called talk-story narrated by one performer, usually over many hours.

Mrs. Han comes out of the shop and we continue along the underground promenade, moving past flocks of shoppers. Near the end of the arcade, we step into Kim Brothers tailors, where the employees snap to attention and bow profusely as Mrs. Han enters—here is real business. Mrs. Han shops for her

husband, four sons, two sons-in-law, and various family employees, and with her, one good suit can lead to another, or,
ten more.

"This is my son-in-law," she says, "a professor and a writer.
Please fit him for a suit and while you do that, let me see your
fabric samples." One of the tailors seats Mrs. Han in an easy
chair and brings out various books of swatches. Another takes
me over to the mirror, where he proceeds to measure every part
of me but my penis. And even that part must be considered.

"Which side you hang from?" he asks.

"What?"

"You know"—he gestures toward his own crotch—"this
side or that side. Right or left."

"Right," I say, "no, left. Well, maybe right. Left. I don't
know."

He studies my crotch. "Left."

"How is it going?" asks Mrs. Han from beyond the gauzy
curtain.

"Oh, fine," I shout. "Everything's going swell."

"Good," she answers, and I see her silhouette return to the
easy chair.

The tailor is a balding, emaciated young man with a cigarette
dangling from his mouth that he removes only when it has
burned down practically to his lip. He looks like a man who
likes to bet on the ponies.

"Big legs," he says, gesturing at my thighs and calves.

"I run a lot," I tell him.

"Ah," he nods. "Long arms, too."

"Used to play basketball."

"Long arms," he says, gesturing like a boxer sparring, "good
to the jab."

"Did that, too," I say.

"Ah"—he nods—"that how come nose all broken up." Then he goes back to his calculations, sighing, frowning, figuring.

"Lotta fabric for you," he says. "We charge more for extra fabric, but Mrs. Han old customer, very good old customer. Many men in her life, husbands, sons, sons-in-law, nothing to worry." He whacks himself on the ass, hard.

"You gotta lotta muscle there," he says. "Need lotta cloth. Need lotta cushion. Protection."

"Whatever," I answer, not sure I've understood the words garbled by the cigarette.

"But you like," he says. "We design suit for Ah-rex-anda Haig. He big all ova, too, and he like Kim Brothers suits excellently."

When I come out of the fitting room, Mrs. Han shows me about seven or eight swatches of cloth and asks which ones I like. I point out one of the gray fabrics, but then she adds five more. I remind her that Haeja has told her that I am to get only one suit.

"That's all right"—Mrs. Han waves off my objection—"it takes so long for you to come to Seoul, let Mother buy a few presents for you."

"I don't really need this many suits," I protest.

"That's all right," she says. "Let Mother buy a few gifts for you."

As we walk back along the arcade toward the Plaza Hotel, I realize that to characterize Mrs. Han as a spendthrift is a misassumption. This seemingly innocuous compulsion to shop and spend, better suited to a matron from a suburb on Long Island, has its roots in the Korean War. The scars of war show, too, in her carefully prepared social face and in the high, thin register of her voice that can sing like a well-strung musical instrument but can fall out of tune at a moment's notice.

As a young woman of privilege and a young bride in an arranged marriage, Mrs. Han was a person for whom *having* was a natural condition of life. ("Having," though, was relative; even the well-off did not have many goods then.) With the war, she suddenly found herself not having for the first time, and needing and wanting. In three years the entire country was devastated, and an entire generation robbed of its native resources and established social order. A can of Spam was a luxury; so was a man. Mrs. Han went from being a child of privilege to a working woman and, more startlingly, from wife of a provincial doctor to mistress of a millionaire.

Now that she does *have,* Mrs. Han does not so much flaunt her wealth as spread it around, among her children, her friends, and to the shops downtown. Instead of one tie, she'll buy me seven or eight; instead of one shirt, ten. Yet hers is less a case of conspicuous consumption than a celebratory gesture, a declaration that she is alive. Any day, her generation believes, the bounty of this earth can be wiped out in a howitzer flash—or, more likely, a nuclear cloud.

War makes its survivors special people, life's ultimate realists. I like Mrs. Han's manner because I think I understand its roots: back in the time of America's initial involvement, the 1950s, when Korea was a long, scarred landscape, and widows roamed like ghosts in the rubble. Having survived not only the war but social censure in its aftermath, she is as tough as the granite mountains in which she has always lived. And like many war survivors, she has made a fairly good life for herself.

. . .

Shopping fever demands that Mrs. Han buy at least a few items of every lot she sees, so I begin to accumulate yet another collection of shirts, ties, and socks. In yet another antique shop, she looks at a celadon vase and asks my opinion.

"Beautiful," I say. She tells the woman to wrap it up.

We pass a jewelry store, and she tells me that Fionna needs a ring. I say that she is too young and will only lose it.

"Just one," Mother says.

"All right," I say, "but only if it is cheap." She buys two gold bands and six or seven painted silver ones.

We rejoin the driver and car in front of the Seoul Plaza, and continue on to Insa-Dong, a mile to the northeast.

The driver leaves us off at the northern end of the long, narrow street lined with art galleries and antique shops. As we work through the crowds and traffic, dealers come out of their shops and bow hello to Mrs. Han, inviting her in to see a screen or a painting, a vase or a Korean chest. In the downtown shops every other person seems to know Mrs. Han, particularly when she has shopping fever; here it is apparent that everyone does.

Finally, we enter one of the shops, where the dealer immediately invites us into the back room. We remove our shoes and sit on the carpeted floor at a low table. Barley tea and a bean-curd cake are served. Mrs. Han explains to me a narrative screen painting hung on the far wall.

It is the story of Tomi, a righteous man of humble birth with a beautiful, virtuous wife. The king hears about this remarkable couple, and invites Tomi to the court. Then the king says that while chastity and purity are the greatest virtues for women, there isn't a woman alive who would not be tempted by clever words whispered in the dark when no one else is around. Tomi disagrees, saying his wife is true unto death.

Such words intrigue the king, who has Tomi detained and the wife summoned. When she arrives, the king tells her that he has heard of her beauty for a long time and desired her, and that he now has won her in a bet with her husband. The art dealer chuckles as he listens, his round belly shaking. The king never lies, says the wife, and when the king invites her to his bedchamber, she seems to obey. Please enter the room first, she says, and I'll change my clothes and follow you. But she sends in a slave girl dressed as herself, and when the king discovers this, he has Tomi's eyes gouged out and his body set adrift in a boat on the river.

I look at the many-paneled screen on the wall, seeing each segment of the story rendered there. Yet it seems incomplete.

"That's the whole story?" I ask.

"The last panels are missing," answers the dealer.

"What is not on the screen," Mrs. Han says, "is that the king tries to rape the wife a second time, but she tells him that she has her period. Let me wait a day, she says, and I'll be yours. Then she escapes, finds her husband, blinded but still alive, and they flee to a foreign land."

Back home, Haeja and her mother are at it again. It seems Mrs. Han wants to buy me still more suits. Haeja is adamant, but there is no arguing with Mrs. Han.

"A few more," she insists.

"None." Haeja repeats.

"All right," her mother says, thin and straight, haughty, at once authoritative and frail. "But if your husband dresses well, he will find a better position at the university. He will publish more books. And if you don't dress like a noble lady, your husband cannot succeed."

"What about *my* career?" her daughter asks.

"Ah," Mother smiles. "Let's be serious. You are a mother now, and a mother must look and act a certain way."

Watching her, Audrey Hepburn comes to mind. Photographs of Mrs. Han from the 1950s suggest that she was aware of the resemblance and played it up in her choice of dress and hairdo. Enter Mr. Han, smoking a cigarette, his face hung like Humphrey Bogart's, pondering the universe.

"We go shop," he says.

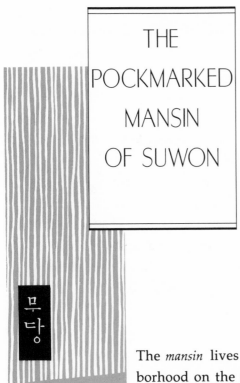

THE POCKMARKED MANSIN OF SUWON

무
당

The *mansin* lives in a ramshackle neighborhood on the outskirts of Suwon, the old fortress city just south of Seoul. Her farmhouse consists of two simple rooms, one of them filled with the arcane objects of her trade, the other bare and spotless. The bare courtyard with several peach trees in flower is framed by an old wall of squared stones topped by concave tiles filled with mortar; a sweet scent fills the air. Out back chickens and geese wander around an enclosure next to a small vegetable garden. The only suggestion that this farmhouse is different from any other in the neighborhood is a pair of totem poles outside the gate.

Probably nothing has changed on the mansin's property in more than a hundred years, except that the thatched roof has been replaced by tin, painted a garish blue-green. Nothing has changed about her profession for much longer. Before Buddha,

Confucius, Lao-tzu, and Jesus, animists plied their trade in Korea. Medium, magician, healer, priestess, the shaman is "one who knows." Some refer to them condescendingly as *mudang,* but the polite term, the one shamans use for themselves, is mansin, meaning "ten thousand spirits," the potential number a good shaman is able to contact.

Here lives Koo Soon-Ja, the Pockmarked Mansin of Suwon, and her spare farmyard exudes the shamanic quality of *um,* of yin, of the feminine. Nearly all a mansin's customers are women, too. Although shamans of other cultures are often men, the few Korean men who do become shamans invariably dress as women for the ceremony, the *kut;* only on Cheju-do, a volcanic island paradise off the southern coast of the peninsula where women are pearl divers and dominate the culture, are men often the shamans.

In times of moderate disorder, a mansin may do only modest business, her customers being more comforted by the great civil order of Confucianism. At times of crisis, however, her customers may pray to Buddha or, more recently, to Christ. When they have doubts, they go to the local fortune-teller. When their children grow up, they seek out matchmakers for weddings. But when all else fails, the country people turn to their animism; they visit the mudang. The Pockmarked Mansin of Suwon is there to help them through illness, cleansings, personal difficulties, and especially trouble with meddlesome ghosts.

Esteemed as her profession may sometimes be, the Pockmarked Mansin knows that her social status is no better than that of a butcher, a prostitute, or a kisaeng. (In the old days actors were put in this social class, too.) When not performing kut, the mansin runs a drinking house down the road, and her customers are mostly farm and factory workers. In fact, two of her assistants, sorcerer's apprentices, are bar girls—prostitutes. To the women of her community, the mansin is a medium; to the men, she is a madame. She chose the latter profession to support herself, because her primary craft brings in money erratically.

The Pockmarked Mansin did not choose to become a shaman, spirits from the beyond chose her. As a young girl, she had dreams of becoming a movie star, a singer, a stage actress, even a pianist. Her father was a magistrate who fell on hard times. The mansin then married against her parents' wishes, choosing a local man from a poor farming family known as leaders of the *pon-sandae,* masked folk-drama plays put on during festivals. He was listed as missing-in-action during the Korean War, and she took up with another poor man who dreamed of becoming a *p'ansori* (talk-story) artist. She loved his gravelly storyteller's voice, but he drank excessively and was not kind to her children. Years later, her husband returned, giving her an excuse to leave the p'ansori singer, who drank more and more, telling stories less and less.

That was when the first migraines appeared, and phantom stomach pains, pains from ghosts shooting along her lower back and legs. She would swell one day, have epileptic fits the next. Some days she wandered around Suwon like a madwoman, muttering to herself, fighting off the possession of her soul by this spirit. Some people said that the war had driven her insane, that the shame of her husband's return had been too much for her. But others recognized the first signs of "the sickness," which she fought for ten years, until she could fight it no longer and had to give in. Then the Pockmarked Mansin of Suwon apprenticed herself to the Bowlegged Mansin of Suwon, who gave her to understand that her real teacher was the spirit who possessed her. She understood.

The Mansin of Suwon learned to see through the veil that the world of phenomena puts up before all of us; she contacted spirits of mountains and rivers, of stones and trees, roots and branches. She became a go-between for her neighbors with the spirit world, an appeaser, a cajoler, a teaser, seducing spirit generals, becoming Tangun's mistress; her powers became a local antidote to the poisons found in nature. In trance states, she entered the hypnotic world that included not only Tangun the Founder, the son of a bear and a heavenly spirit, but also other warriors, witches, the three generals of the five directions, and zodiacal beasts. She adopted rituals and ceremonies from other sources for her own ends, drawing upon Buddhism, Confucianism, Taoism, and even Christianity, kneading these beliefs into an animistic concoction. The ghost of a previous Pockmarked Shaman of Suwon, this one a Koguryo shaman who had advised the ancient kings about war and prosperity, was Virgil to her Dante.

The Pockmarked Mansin is nowhere to be seen yet, but in the yard a table is laid with her costumes and paraphernalia for the kut. The woman who has arranged for the ceremony is already present. She hopes to heal her ailing husband, a potter who has not worked for half a year. He suffers from chronic stomachaches that neither conventional nor folk doctors have been able to cure or explain. The wife is a dressmaker, a small, dark, silent woman of great mystery. Several members of our family have been invited to the ceremony as her guests.

She leads Byung-Jeen and me along the side of the farmhouse to a little porch in the back, where her husband sits drinking maggoli, rice wine, smoking cigarettes, and playing solitaire. She introduces us but he only grunts a brusque *an-yong-ha-sae-yo,* pours us glasses of rice wine and goes back to his cards. It is clear that he sees no solution for his stomach, certainly not through a shaman ceremony in Suwon. He drinks off the maggoli and pours himself another one; it occurs to me that if he cut back on the cigarettes and rice wine his stomachaches would probably go away.

A string of recent events has brought me to Suwon. One afternoon, on the way to visit Grandma Oh, Haeja and I stopped to watch a shaman perform a cleansing ceremony at the shell of an office building going up on Samchung-dong, right across from the entrance to the Hans' house. I was fascinated, of course, but Haeja could provide me with few details about the craft. Then her stepsister Byung-Soon asked me to read an essay on shamanism she was writing for her applications to several American colleges. And sitting in the kitchen one day a few weeks ago, while talking with Haeja and Byung-Soon about shamans, I had a few words with the dressmaker, who was waiting for Mrs. Han.

Dressmakers, greengrocers, fishmongers, fortune-tellers—these are just a few of the tradespeople who regularly come to the back door of the house. There were probably five or six dressmakers alone, but this one was a favorite of Haeja and her sisters, who had known her since childhood. Now she had her own dress business, and traveled from Suwon to Seoul several times a month to visit clients.

"Do you remember that summer you took us from Taegu to the beach at Pusan?" Haeja asked.

The woman did not say anything.

"You remember," Haeja said, "that summer when every day was over a hundred degrees."

Somehow, the little dark woman conveyed affirmation without nodding or speaking.

I was questioning Byung-Soon about shamans again when

the dressmaker spoke. It was the first time I had ever heard a word from her, even though I must have seen her in the kitchen ten times before.

"She said that she has a friend who knows the Pockmarked Mansin of Suwon, a very famous shaman, a woman of incredible spiritual gifts. If you like, she will speak to her friend about letting us attend a kut." I heard nothing more about the invitation for over a week. Then one evening Haeja told me that a visit to the Pockmarked Mansin had been arranged. The next day, several of us drove down to Suwon in two cars. Mrs. Han, a great believer in fortune-tellers, stayed home, castigating us for this foolish interest in a mere mudang.

Instead of concrete, as in courtyards in Seoul, the yard is of pounded dirt, a parched amber brown before the monsoon season.

Often the priestess comes to the house of the sick, but the dressmaker rents a small room in a distant relative's house down the road, and it would be inappropriate—not to mention too crowded—for all of us to gather there. Instead, it had been decided to hold the kut at the mansin's home, so the dressmaker has brought the shaman various articles belonging to her husband—his pipe, his whiskey glass, his lighter, a pair of his shoes, a pair of trousers, a workshirt, his lucky coin, and several of the finest vases from his kiln. About half of the Pockmarked Mansin's kut are held on these premises.

If the dressmaker were more affluent, several more apprentice shamans would attend the mansin. If she were even poorer than she is, perhaps only the shaman herself would perform the ceremony. Or maybe the kut would be held simultaneously with several others. If the party is really poor, Pockmarked Mansin simply calls up one of her assistants and gives her the business. The dressmaker isn't really well off enough to afford the two assistants plus the shaman; either the priestess is giving her neighbor a break or the dressmaker is spending beyond her means, for face or for show—not a rare phenomenon in Korea.

I have been instructed in advance about how to behave. The outside social world still centers on males and male-oriented Confucian values and ceremonies, but the kut is very much a woman's world; the mansin may invoke female ancestors, and there is some concern that the presence of a man may distract her. On top of that, I am an American, and while these country people have probably seen their share of American soldiers, few have had Americans in their homes.

I have been told to go off with Byung-Jeen and the husband for a few minutes, but when the ceremony begins, we may creep around the side of the house and watch from this hidden perch. The husband does not react when we stand and steal along the wall of the house to the edge of the building. Grandma Oh sees me, though, and smiles and waves, but Hae-Soon pulls down her hand before the mansin can see. Byung-Jeen seems as bored as the husband and wanders back to join him. When I look back, I see that they have begun a game of Go.

Now the mansin appears in a long, flowing outfit, a sinewy figure in red, taller than any of the other women—in fact, nearly my own height. I have been told that she is fifty-five years old, but she looks maybe twenty years younger than that. Despite her nickname, she is a striking-looking woman. She does not wear any makeup, and her skin, though scarred by acne, is pale and without wrinkles. Her cheeks are plump, as if filled with nuts, and she has a certain chipmunklike beauty. She wears a hat with a flat, black brim and stiff red peak, like Zorro's or a flamenco dancer's. The tools of her trade lie around the courtyard: bells, drum, a machetelike knife, cigarettes, a white hood, and other costumes that she will change into, depending on which of the ten thousand spirits takes possession of her in this matter of the ailing husband and his poor stomach.

Part actress and physician's assistant, con artist, seductress, earth-woman, enchantress, devil-worshiper, faith healer, purveyor of elixirs, divine, magistrate, go-go queen, cock teaser, mistress, general, sword-swallower, fire-eater, animal tamer, and also part poor woman lacking formal education, part chanteuse, dancer, musician, tiger trainer, the mansin prepares for the ceremony in the courtyard.

The dressmaker stands center-stage with a handful of paper money to appease the various spirits. "I know it is the ghost of his first wife," she says anxiously.

"Silence," says the mansin, and the courtyard goes quiet.

In preparing for the kut, the spirits have to be considered. River and mountain spirits can be difficult at times. Animal spirits are invoked—the deer, the tortoise, the magpie, the pig, this last often wild and skittish. The mansin has to worry about spiders, too, a sign of bad luck. A good kut can be ruined by the intrusion of a spider.

That is why her yard has peach trees. The flowers and branches bring good luck, as do the totem poles outside the courtyard and the red posts in front of the house. That's why she herself wears red, and why her home is spotless, the floors and even the patios without a speck of dirt. A clean house invites good spirits and turns away evil ones.

Dead souls are everywhere in Suwon. Through the various dynasties the old fortress town has accumulated its share of good and bad spirits. People died in battles here, some in evil ways, their ghosts still not appeased. Often the meddlesome spirit of her first husband's mother, by the p'ansori singer's daughter or even by the spirit of her own firstborn, a crib death, have interrupted her kut.

Tangun, the founder of Korea, has a special fondness for Pockmarked Mansin. Often he possesses her, and when he does, her ceremonies always go well. It has been some time since Tangun has come down from his mountain to visit her, and today seems auspicious for a visit from him. He would be a good healer for this old man; Tangun understands the nature of the Korean stomach best of all the ten thousand spirits. With him, there are always bear and tiger spirits, oxen, river dragons, fox, deer, rabbits, even good snakes.

The mansin has asked us to become more sensitive to the spirit world around us, or at least to suspend our disbelief. Haeja, Hae-Soon, and Byung-Soon, I notice, stand out as city slickers in this country yard. Only Grandma Oh projects the right attitude, her excitement giving way to seriousness.

The shaman's assistants get to work. Rice cake, fruit, chickens, a steaming pig's head are marched into the yard. A gentle breeze stirs the surrounding pines. As though on cue, the rumblings of the city beyond seem to go mute. Outside the courtyard and down the road, I hear the soft music of children's voices, laughing and giggling, in the afternoon air. Everything gives off an air of expectation, like a barometric drop just before a storm.

Food and wine are placed at the gate, which stands open. The drum is readied. "Out, out!" the mansin shouts, and several maids and assistants come from the back of the house, where the kitchen is. The drum beats, awakening the spirits of the house. My heartbeat accelerates slightly, it seems like that strange moment before the lights come up in a theater. Cymbals and drums collide as two assistants play. The mansin knows which mountains and rivers house good and bad spirits in these parts, where to drive some spirits off and where to invite others.

The mansin looks even younger as she writhes and gyrates, possessed of her spirits. She bounces on her toes, dancing around, arms flailing; her energy seems bottomless. Her lips pucker as though in a kiss. The next instant, she is scowling, her eyebrows knitting together. She runs over and puts on a different-colored vest over the red outfit. Her flamenco hat has been knocked back with all the jumping around, but it has not fallen to the ground because it is tied under her chin and so rides on her back. Her words spew out in a stream of hisses and coos, and I wish Haeja were nearby to tell me what is being said.

I get the feeling that she is doing battle with one of her personal spirits, a visitor who frequently comes bearing trouble at the beginning of kut, but one she knows how to cajole or drive off. Then, as suddenly as the ghostly presence possessed her, it departs, and the shaman seems to have taken on a gruff, manly spirit intent on belittling the tiny, dark dressmaker. She appears frightened, but hands over the bills. Perhaps this is one of the greedy generals—the Knife-Wielding General, General Lightning-Bolt, General White-Horse, the Fire General, the Horse General of the Red-Dirt—who possesses the shamans in their trances. He is not easily satisfied, and demands vast quantities of food, money, homage, and respect. Poor families have lost everything to shamans possessed by this wicked ghost.

"Give him some more money," Grandma Oh calls from the rear. "Go ahead, give him a few more won. That greedy bastard general only knows money. Give him a few more won and be done with him."

The corrupting male spirit has disappeared, mollified by the offering, but now the mansin flings the food from the table around the yard, like a crazy woman in a fit. She does not speak, does not chant, but sputters and spews and growls like a wild animal. Let the hungry, thirsty spirits all around the courtyard get their fill immediately, they will be less distracting later. With other scraps of food, the mansin divines, pointing here, walking there, studying, thinking, growling, sucking, hissing. Again, things quiet down quickly. She changes into another costume with rainbow sleeves and a peaked hat.

The assistants drum and bang their cymbals, moving onto the porch of the house, where the ailing husband's personal items are laid out on a low table. As the women move toward the house and the shaman chants and sings the kut, her crazy face reminds me of a redheaded Irish aunt with a bottle of whiskey in her, friendly one second, in a rage the next; moments later, sweet and kind, then turning furious, ready to kill. Suddenly I'm unsettled, tense, anxious, uncertain.

Quieter, the mansin performs an ablution to rid filthy spirits from the husband's possessions. I turn to look at the man himself, barely able to keep his head straight because he's drunk so much rice wine already. The mansin sprinkles a liquid around the porch, then slivers of red peppers and other foods. Who cleans up after the ceremony? I wonder.

The mansin comes out of her trance momentarily and drinks some wine, wiping her brow.

"Ah, good," she says, then immediately falls back into the ecstatic trance.

First, there was Heaven, Earth, and the Twelve Kings of the Underworld. This was before Buddha, before Confucius, before Christ, before Humans even, when the universe was divided into three nether regions. Like today, the destiny of Earth was oriented toward five directions: north, south, east, west, and center. All natural objects possessed souls. The sun, the moon, the stars were gods, animals were kings. Then came Tangun. The Pockmarked Mansin of Suwon has met once again with her great spirit, the founder of Korea, a spirit that bodes well for the ailing husband at the side of the house. I am told that when Tangun possesses the shaman, her cleansings and healings work absolutely. But even when this benign spirit of bear and Heaven inhabits the mansin, she must journey through time to bring him into her courtyard. She must reach back into the spirits of prehistory and guide her master to this present world.

"Hwannung," she calls, invoking the heavenly spirit who fathered Tangun, "come down from Mount Paektusan with your horde of spirits, visit your friend the Pockmarked Shaman. Lay the twenty beads of garlic and wormwood for the tiger and the bear. Let them hibernate in a cave for twenty days. Transform the bear into a beautiful woman—make love to her, Hwannung, so that you may bring forth Tangun, the father of our country, the founder and leader of the spirit world. Let him fly across time to this purified offering in the farmyard of the Mansin of Suwon, the pockmarked woman with the body of a young girl." Here she wiggles and writhes, her tongue darting out of her mouth.

"Naughty girl," Grandma Oh says, laughing.

Haeja and Hae-Soon hush her.

Like a go-go dancer in a hot nightclub act, the mansin wraps her long legs around one of the poles in front of her house and grinds her pelvis into it, moaning and calling Tangun's name.

"Perhaps Tangun has taken up with the Big-Breasted Shaman of Taejon," one of the assistants says, giggling.

"Quiet," the other assistant hisses.

"Silence," the shaman herself says from her trance.

Her shouts and screams come louder and faster and she has what seems like a climax.

Everyone whispers what a good sign this is, that Tangun has not only descended on the mansin and possessed her, but has deigned to make love to her. The shaman continues to writhe and moan like a cat in heat, the possession a veritable fountain of youth. But as quickly as Tangun took her, she becomes another ghost, this one a screaming, shouting shrew. She changes into a white hooded costume.

"His first wife," the dressmaker whispers fearfully. But it is not the first wife—it is his last mistress, it seems, and she is very greedy for the cash that the potter used to lavish on her. He had to make many vases and urns to entertain this bawdy old kisaeng with her insatiable appetite for sex, money, food, and drink. The mansin picks up a beautiful celadon vase with many cranes etched on it and lifts it over her head, as though to smash it to pieces.

"Wait!" the dressmaker screams, stuffing larger denominations of won into the pig's ears, nostrils, and mouth. She is unaware of the ghost's identity until the mansin tells her, in a husky, boozey voice. Immediately the wife tries to retrieve the money from the pig's orifices, but the mansin warns her that if the mistress is not appeased, she will continue to wreak her fury on the poor husband's stomach. Reluctantly the dressmaker puts back the money and adds a little more.

"Better, better," the shaman whispers in her husky voice, then undulates full-hipped around the courtyard, plumping up her breasts, dancing like a young girl in a disco.

"Where is my lover?" she demands.

"Out back," the assistants shout at once.

117

"Bring him to me," she shouts.

I whisper to Byung-Jeen to bring the drunken old man up front. The man stumbles headlong into the courtyard, unaware of the presence of this spirit. The mansin pours wine, and I remember that when wine is offered in this type of possession a man must be present to accept it.

But the mansin is a master of the dramatic, and she dances around the courtyard first, full of a new surge of sexual fury. Instead of offering the wine to the potter, she proffers it to Byung-Jeen, who waves her off. Then she spots me and gestures me toward a low table in the center of the yard.

"What am I supposed to do?" I ask Haeja.

"Drink it," she says. "You have no trouble drinking, do you?"

I squat and drink the wine; it is sweet and sour and leaves a chalky aftertaste. The drums beat louder in my ears, the cymbals go faster. Before I can stand up, the mansin jumps on my shoulders, driving her pelvis into my neck, shouting names and places, curses and prayers, her possession approaching insanity.

"Get off him!" Grandma Oh shouts, almost like a spectator at a wrestling match. "Get the fuck off Michael Sa-bong, you old whore, and give the wine to your potter friend over there!" This is only a setup, it turns out, and the mansin quickly dismounts from my back and offers wine to the drunken potter, who lurches for her breasts, oblivious to his wife standing a few feet away.

"Do you know my name?" the mansin asks coquettishly.

"You are the Pockmarked Mansin," the potter laughs.

"Wrong!" she shouts. She puts down the wine, runs over to her table and comes back with a tridentlike pitchfork and the huge machetelike knife, which she whips through the air so furiously that I fear for her control and step out of the way.

"You dirty bastard!" the mansin screams. "Fuck me and take advantage of me and don't even leave any money for my funeral or put flowers on my gravestone, never visit me or make offerings for my well-being in the afterlife!"

Still the man does not realize whose ghost this is, or maybe he just doesn't care. The mansin lets the sword and the trident drop to her sides. She comes toward him a step at a time, leading with her right foot, dragging the left. Somehow she makes this crippled dance very erotic.

"My little pumpkin," she coos. "My little *sabong-nim,* my little *yabo.* "

With these words the potter trembles and drops the glass of wine and the color bleaches out of his face.

"My Little Peony Flower," he says incredulously.

"My Little Peony Flower?" the dressmaker asks.

"Dirty bastard," Grandma Oh mutters. The Oh sisters are struck dumb. The kut is better than the Korean soap operas on afternoon television.

"Peony Flower," the man says, taking the wine, guzzling so fast that it drools down the side of his mouth.

"I'll kill you," the wife says.

"Where have you been?" the man asks his mistress.

"I'm horny," the mansin growls, "I'm hungry, I'm broke, I'm cold, I need a new dress, I'm thirsty. . . ."

The man's hands tremble so much that when he pours wine for the thirsty ghost, half of it spills on the ground. She is hungry, too, so he runs over and brings back some rice cakes.

"Here," he says, no longer the disinterested bystander.

The mansin gorges herself on rice cake and drinks wine like a steelworker. She rubs herself over the potter, then mounts him from behind. Her assistants drape the potter with some of his own clothing, and the mansin drapes the white cape over him, rattling her sword near the covered form.

"This one's a home wrecker," Grandma Oh mutters. "I know the type, I know the type. Just like that woman who ran off with my husband."

Again, the Pockmarked Mansin of Suwon grinds herself into the man's neck, only this time she is not dismounting until she is satisfied, first with her pleasures, then with some hard cash.

She moans, building to another climax, and mutters, "I need cash, pumpkin. I need money for a new dress."

"I'm broke, darling."

"Hasn't your stomach told you of my needs, pumpkin?"

"He hasn't worked in half a year," the dressmaker shouts. "He's sick, leave him alone, you old whore."

"Tell her," Grandma Oh agrees.

"You stinking whore!" the dressmaker screams, "Get off my husband!"

"Money, money, money," the mansin intones, gyrating on the potter's back. "Money, money, money."

"I'm broke," the potter says.

"Your wife is hiding money under her skirt," the mansin says.

"Dirty, filthy bitch," the dressmaker mutters, pulling up her skirt and taking money from a pouch strapped to her thigh. She flings the money toward the husband.

"This is why your children did not receive a good education," she curses, "because you were spending all your money on this rotten whore." He scoops up the money in his hands, denying nothing. After the mansin peaks, she dismounts and counts the money. This is not enough to cure the potter's stomach, she says, in the voice of the last mistress. She is a woman of many tastes and appetites. The wife hands her husband a wad of bills.

"Where did you get this money from?" he asks.

"Never mind where I got anything," she scolds him.

"This is not dressmaking money," he says.

"Never mind," she scolds.

The mansin pulls down the front of her dress, beckoning the potter to place the bills in her cleavage, which he gladly does. When he is near enough, she pulls him on top of her, mashing his face in her breasts.

"What a cheap whore," the dressmaker sighs. "What a foolish man to destroy his family over this slut."

"Home wrecker," Grandma Oh spits. "I know the type, I know her type, all right."

The two assistants have lost their concentration and seem as bewildered as the onlookers by this mistress ghost.

Suddenly the mansin pushes the potter away.

"Go, go," she says, pointing him back toward the side of the house. "Out of my sight, unfaithful lover."

"How's your stomach?" the wife asks sarcastically as he turns to go.

"Jo-ah, jo-ah," he says in a little mouse voice. "Fine, fine."

It is getting late, and Haeja points to her watch, signaling me that it is time to go. I slip over to join the women, and one of the assistants comes to us.

"We break for supper," she says, "please stay for a meal."

"We must get back to Seoul," Hae-Soon says.

The second part of the kut may last deep into the night, even into the morning. Sometimes, I have heard, a kut may last for days, with the participants pausing only for meals and other bodily needs.

Grandma Oh walks over to the mansin, who sits on the steps

to the house, smoking a cigarette and drinking wine. She hands the shaman money, and I guess she is asking about her son, if his spirit is warm, or maybe about her errant husband.

Haeja and Hae-Soon join her and Grandma Oh tells them, "She says that both of you have good fortune."

The shaman tells them that a doctor not related to this other family or ceremony was at the gate during the kut, begging to come in and be heard.

"My son," Grandma Oh says proudly.

"And there were other spirits," the mansin says, dragging hard on her cigarette. She pinches out the ember and field-strips the cigarette, scattering the tobacco and paper through the yard. "One carried a big pen and was a foreigner. The other was a drowned sailor with a bald head."

The sisters and Grandma Oh look to me for an answer, but I can't imagine who these spirits could be.

"Maybe some great writer who has adopted me," I say in English, laughing.

"No, no," the shaman answers in Korean, though she understands no English. "These are your relatives."

We say good-bye. Grandma Oh gives the mansin more money, for a ceremony, and takes away several strips of red paper. The dressmaker is screaming at her drunken husband, who has returned to his game of solitaire. Byung-Jeen joins us and we go to the cars parked near the gate.

After the meal, the kut will continue. Perhaps some other household demons will need appeasement, although the main culprit of the stomachache seems to have been located.

On the drive north to Seoul I'm struck by an awareness, which I tell Haeja about. My great-grandfather Richard McCann was a writer, a journalist in New York City around the turn of the century. A Columbia dropout, he was disowned by his father for giving up his faith, living out of wedlock, and taking up writing instead of law. He wrote a book called *The War Horror,* a tract against World War I, which he believed was started to make money for industrialists.

Haeja tells her grandmother.

"That's it," Grandma Oh says. "A good thing it wasn't one of those tramps like that Peony Flower. *Aigo,* the poor dressmaker."

"What about the bald sailor?" my wife asks me, but I have no answer, no clues, no idea who that other foreign spirit might be.

Mountains give way to cityscape, and Seoul appears on the horizon as the sun goes down. We drive across the Han River and northward through the city to home.

"Aigo," sighs Grandma Oh.

The next morning, waking from sleep, I remember. I had a bald-headed uncle who was a sailor; he lived with my family on Long Island when he was back in port. He was one of my mother's younger brothers, an adventurer who had been all over the world, and as children we marveled at his stories about Africa, Europe, South America, Australia, and Asia. One of my first traumas was learning of his death; he drowned while working as a bursar on a merchant ship. He had signed on to run resupply ships from the United States to American soldiers in Korea during the war, and was swept overboard off the coast of Pusan, in southeastern Korea, during a monsoon. His body was never recovered.

"The other spirit," I tell Haeja, "was my Uncle Billy," and then I tell her about this relative I haven't thought to mention until now.

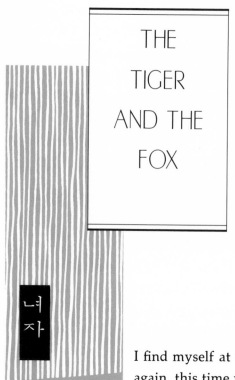

THE
TIGER
AND THE
FOX

여자

I find myself at the hub of the city once
again, this time working my way toward
Sejong-ro so I can walk northward home.
Duk-Soo Palace, the Seoul Plaza Hotel, and City Hall fan out
on three sides of the big plaza at the center of the city, and I
descend into the Bando Arcade to get to City Hall.

Earlier in the day I had gone to the bookshop on Chongno,
one of the large cross streets that run east to west through the
northern part of the city. On the fifth floor were Korean books
in English. Maybe because my first eyes and ears on the peninsula were Haeja's, I've become interested in the role of Korean
women in history and literature, and I was in search of books
about them.

In Korea, men flaunt power; women finesse theirs. Where
men yell, women whisper to make their points. There are no
secrets in the *chaebol,* the giant conglomerates, the ultimate

124

man's place. But the feminine place of business, lunch with the ladies at the regular *gae,* the investment gatherings, are built on secrets, on the salting away of large sums of money as each member takes her turn to collect the bounty invested over the years. Whenever I ask Hae-Soon about the *gae,* she smiles, says, *"Morogo?"* What? she asks, and when Haeja asks for my benefit, her sister smiles again, this time laughing, but never answering us.

Beyond being mother and wife, a Korean woman can be one of only a handful of other things, and fundamentally she is considered either a tiger or a fox. If she is fierce, she is a tiger; if cunning, a fox. The notion of the fox comes from Chinese folklore, which is full of tales in which that animal transforms itself into a beautiful woman who seduces men and then kills them. The tiger is more characteristic to the Korean folktales. If a woman is called a fox, she is attractive, seductive, wily, and dangerous. But if she is a tiger, she is fierce, impatient, and warriorlike. There is an element of androgyny in the tiger image. Though it was the Siberian tiger that roamed the mountains of Korea, the creature in folk paintings is really no bigger than a lynx, and has huge amber eyes like a domestic cat.

In the legend about the founding of Korea, when Hwannung descends to earth with three thousand spirits, a tiger and a bear visit him and ask for the mountain secrets. Hwannung tells them that if they want the secrets, they must first eat the miraculous wormwood stalk with twenty beads of garlic and then hide in a cave for twenty-one days. But the tiger becomes impatient and stalks off. When the bear emerges from the cave, it is transformed into a woman, and in the year 2333 B.C., Tangun, the first king of Korea, is born to Hwannung and the bear. It is from this legend that the tiger gained the reputation of being an impatient, warriorlike creature.

In the Yi dynasty, the yangban class consisted of nobles and officers. The symbol signifying the former was a crane or, if the noble was really highborn, two cranes. For the military the symbol was a tiger patch worn on the chest of the officer's outer coats. A two-tiger general was a truly great warrior. It was during the Yi dynasty that the division of the sexes became pervasive, and many of the inequities suffered by women originates in that period. Prior to the neo-Confucianist Yi dynasty, Korea had periods when women not only prevailed as the equals of men but actually outdid them, and at times becoming dominant.

During the Yi dynasty, women were thought of as dutiful, humble beings. Their finest role was as mothers; outside the home, they were generally laborers or sex objects. In this century, the old order has been changed by a few female doctors, professors, and lawyers, tigerlike women who have fought their way to the top. But everyone in Seoul has a story about a woman who was not a tiger, but rather a fox; invariably she is an attractive, sexy woman who seduced her way to success and esteem. Then there are the martyrs, women like Yoo Kwan-Soon, Korea's Joan of Arc, who opposed the Japanese earlier in this century.

Today, however, Seoul is populated by a new generation of women who find the roles of such female types constraining and meaningless. College-age women, like my younger sisters-in-law, have no intention whatsoever of following the old rules about proper female conduct in the social realm. They want to emulate women like the violinist Kyung-Hwa Chung, who transcend gender and type by virtue of an enormous talent.

The women's rejection of the old stereotypes isn't surprising, given the second-class status so long conferred on them.

During the Yi dynasty a woman could never disobey her parents-in-law; she had to bear a son; she was forbidden to commit adultery. Her husband could divorce her for any infractions of these rules, and also if she showed jealousy, carried a hereditary disease, was garrulous, or committed larceny. Of course, residues of these so-called evils persist today. A young wife's mother-in-law is still her most difficult relative; the importance of having male heirs cannot be slighted, even though people try to downplay it now. Adultery is still grounds for divorce, just as it is nearly everywhere else in the world, though an adulterous male has a lot more license in Korea than he would have elsewhere.

A good, traditional woman still shows piety toward parents, warm concern for siblings, reverence to ancestors, and conceals her own emotions and opinions. What separates her from her Yi maternal forebears, who also believed in such conduct, is that they were forbidden to play harmless games or indulge in any amusement that might have broken the monotony of their lives. An Yi woman was not permitted on the street during daylight. After nine o'clock at night, when men were banned from the streets, she could go out, provided she covered her face with her skirts if she was a commoner, or with a black veil if she was a noblewoman. Today people's given names are rarely used; instead one is referred to by a title, so-and-so's daughter, wife, mother, sister. But in the Yi period, women literally had no given names but only those associative titles. Legally, the paternal side of the family was paramount, and social status and rights were transmitted from fathers to sons. Only the illegitimate were more keenly discriminated against than women.

One in a million of the Yi women managed to achieve a sovereignty of sorts in the bedchambers of China or Japan.

Empress Chi of the Yuan dynasty of China, for example, came to the court from Koryo as a slave. The eunuch Ko Yong-bo, a Korean, helped her in her journey, and introduced her to Emperor Shun-ti as a tea server. The king took a liking to her, and she quickly became his consort. When the empress became jealous, the emperor had her banished for treason. But because the emperor could have as his primary spouse only a woman from a particular family, Lady Chi became the second empress. When the first empress died, Lady Chi assumed the throne, but she reigned for only a year before she was driven out in a Mongol coup and returned to Korea with her son, and the eunuch.

The most difficult periods for women were during the Manchu and Japanese invasions early in the Yi dynasty when the cost of remaining chaste was often one's life. Yi women carried a *changdo,* a ceremonial knife, to ward off attackers, usually Japanese or Ming soldiers. During the Japanese invasion of the late sixteenth century, hundreds of Korean women killed themselves rather than face dishonor. In the next century, Manchu invaders carried off thousands of Korean women as spoils of war but often discarded them on the frontiers; when these women returned to the peninsula, they were treated as outcasts.

The ancient Greeks might have gone to battle over Helen, but many of the wars of Korea seem to have been motivated by an attempt to protect its women from outsiders. The Mongol court in China often demanded up to a thousand beautiful Korean women at a time as tribute; invading Japanese, centuries later, took Korean women as concubines. The kisaeng Kyewolhyang became the mistress of General Konishi Yuinaga during the Japanese occupation in the sixteenth century. One night she stole into her Japanese lover's chamber with General

Kim Ung-So and slit Konishi's throat. A tarnished woman—not because of murder, but because she had slept with a Japanese officer—she then asked General Kim to behead her.

In *The Records of Lighted Bramble,* an eighteenth-century court document, King Yongjo of the Yi dynasty writes of how the counsel of his mistress Yongbin, "Bright Princess," saved the state during a time of crisis. But countless other women go unnamed, their stories untold.

Instead of coming out around Sejong-ro, I take a wrong turn and emerge from the underground arcade crowded with shoppers onto a narrow, winding street bursting with people and cars. Oh, Christ, I think, lost again. But this time I don't panic; I scrutinize the unfamiliar buildings and realize from the maggoli and octopus houses, cheap student hangouts, that I am in Moo-Gyo-dong.

Part of being a good husband, father, and son-in-law means I should not get lost again in Seoul, but that is sometimes the only way for me to experience Korea away from the overprotectiveness of Haeja's family. When they are not too carefully watching out for my well-being, they are often too caught up in the pride of being Korean, in wanting to show their Western relative an airbrushed, charming side of Seoul. When I get lost in Seoul I realize how odd my own experience of this country must be compared with that of an American soldier or missionary stationed here, or even the businessmen whose points of contact are nightlife at Walker Hill outside the city and the glitzy downtown hotels. But even at the upscale heart of this city which beats with the intense striving to be *Chae-Il,* Number One, Seoul is funky and gritty.

Taking the mountains as a compass point, I work northward. I follow a group of university students into a *tabang.* Each teahouse I've gone into seems to have a theme reflected in the decor. This one is cool and jazzy, with a glossy, hi-tech atmosphere of polished chrome, pastel-colored walls, and track lighting, with Duke Ellington playing softly in the background. I order a cup of coffee and a pastry from a cart, light a cigarette, and open my shoulder bag to take out one of the books I had bought.

When I look up, I notice three college-age women—moon-faced, with beautiful Mongolian cheekbones delicately rouged—staring at me in wonder. Their male companions smoke incessantly and pay no attention to them. The waitress comes over.

"Copi?"

"Yes," I answer. "More coffee, please."

One wall of the tabang is a replica of the royal sun and moon screen found in the Throne Room of Kyung-Bok Palace. Images of fertility and long life abound on the screen—mushrooms, deer, spindrift and foam of breaking waves, leaping fish, evergreens.

"Bang?" asks the waitress. She holds up a tray piled with rolls, pastry, and tiny loaves of bread.

"No bread," I say, "thank you."

She bows and backs away, a smile on her lips, eyes lowered.

The three coeds are whispering and talking and looking in my direction. I try to concentrate on my book. When I look up again, Uncle Mo stands in front of me.

"Michael!" he shouts, and sits down. "Don't tell me you are lost again."

"Sort of," I answer sheepishly.

"Well, it is good to see you," he says. "I've been so busy that I haven't seen you in weeks."

Since helping the Hans with their recalcitrant neighbor, the tree-cutting general, he has stopped by the house frequently, and he's been the only male regularly willing to escort me around. The other men are working, or are still too shy and uncomfortable with me, or their poor English makes us uncomfortable with one another. So far it has been easier to interact with the women.

The first time Uncle Mo and I went anywhere together he took me to a driving range north of Samchung Mountain. There were only two topics that he seemed willing to discuss with me: the superiority of Kyong-Sang province over Cholla, and women. Like many Korean men, he seemed to believe that American men had a different perception of women. The standard belief was that a Korean woman who married an American never had to do housework, though Haeja could certainly have set them straight.

When I got out of the car, two young girls jogged over to get the golf bag and our shoes from the trunk of the car. We changed our shoes in the "clubhouse," a dirty little room with lockers and a concrete floor that smelled like a men's room, its walls covered with old golfing memorabilia, stained photographs of Arnold Palmer and Jack Nicklaus, and a display case with golf balls, clubs, and Orlon sweaters and golf pants in hideous pastel colors for sale.

I expected to find some kind of facsimile of the driving range of my childhood, an old potato field the size of several football fields, flat as a pancake, with chicken wire at the perimeter to keep the balls on the course. Instead, we came out of the clubhouse onto the driving tees, which gave out on a vantage at the top of the mountain. But for the distant flags that dotted the hillside, the endless expanse called to mind the vistas depicted in screen paintings of rivers and mountains. The tees dropped off precipitously into the side of the hill, working downward into a steep, picturesque ravine. Young girls walked slantwise, like billygoats, shagging golf balls, some of them wearing football-like helmets to protect them from being hit, while others were clad in futuristic outfits of chicken wire and plywood.

Uncle Mo insisted that I use his driver first. We were about the same height, so that the shaft of the club was just right for me. I bent over, took a golf ball and lined it up on the rubber tee in the grass mat.

"Don't bother with that," he said, "the girl will take care of the ball for you." A small girl with a sunburnt face, her head wrapped in a bandanna, scurried over with a small wooden stool, which she set down next to the bucket of balls. As soon as I sliced the first one off into the ravine, she replaced it with another.

"Just like home," said Uncle Mo, beaming.

"Not quite," I answered, uncomfortable with the girl so close to the downswing of the club. If the club struck her hand. . . .

Uncle Mo struck his ball, and the young girl next to him teed up another, hunched over the bucket, her body inches away from the arc of his swing.

WHACK!

Between strokes, he resumed a lecture he'd been giving me on the fate of Korean women.

"Through various Mongol invasions, the nomadic streak of Yuan princesses invaded our gene pool."

WHACK!

"Princess Cheguktang, the daughter of Kublai Khan, rode around Korea as though she were the ruler of the land, making trips to monasteries, and even several trips back to China. She hunted, went on picnics, had parties, even was a sightseer."

WHACK!

"Wealthy Koreans hid their daughters from the Mongols, who would ship them back to China. Or the young girls' heads were shaved to make them look unattractive. Or they substituted widows in disguise, or the wives of criminals, monks' mistresses, kisaeng, shamans, any woman but their daughters."

WHACK! The girl had pulled her bony, red fingers out of the way just in time.

When the second bucket of balls was used up, Uncle Mo flung his club at the girl, whipped off his leather glove and tossed it to her, and motioned for me to follow him to the clubhouse.

"That was good," he said, putting his arm around my shoulder. Inside the shack, a group of men stood around, putting across a synthetic green. More young women hurried about with trays of drinks.

"Write about the women," said Uncle Mo, "but always remember that Korea is a great country for men."

In the tabang, Uncle Mo picks up the book I'm reading and peruses it offhandedly, looking at the photos.

"Look," I say, turning to the notes in the back of the book. "Haeja's Tiger Grandma—Lady Hwang, I mean—is mentioned as one of the first Korean women to be formally educated."

He laughs. "Tiger Grandma," he says. "Only Haeja would call her that."

He laughs again from deep down in his belly. For a moment his eyes take on that thousand-yard stare I've seen countless times on combat veterans, the blank, merciless stare that comes from reading treeline and surviving on instinct alone. Then he comes out of it and takes out a cigarette, offers me one, lights them both, and exhales, sitting back with a sigh, as if an enormous weight has been removed from his shoulders.

"Your wife is the most critical of Lady Hwang in all the family," he says, "and I am the most uncritical."

"Haeja once said that her maternal grandmother would have made a good dictator."

"Ah, yes," he sighs, exhaling smoke. "Lady Hwang was a true diplomat, the first liberated woman of her time." I know from Mrs. Han a bit about Uncle Mo's fascination with her mother. Uncle Mo's mother was not only a legendary beauty but a great singer, who at one time worked for Lady Hwang, but that was not the whole story. His mother was a renowned kisaeng in her day, the mistress of a well-known patriot, and Uncle Mo was the illegitimate progeny of that romance. But a kisaeng's career ended early, at perhaps thirty, and Lady Hwang, though a woman known for her ferocity, had a fondness for the old kisaeng and not only gave her work, though she was withering away on opium, but invited her to her home for parties.

Haeja had her own theories about all of this. Out of earshot of her own mother, she said that the Tiger Lady hung around with ex-kisaeng because her own origins were quite humble— she had been the only child of a poor, ugly seamstress. Just as is true today, education and discipline had been her escape from poverty. But she had married a doctor who wrote poetry, womanized, and died young.

Uncle calls the waitress over and orders coffee and a pastry. His manner with her is gruff and officious, almost bullying.

134

When she leaves, he resumes his more detached, rather scholarly manner.

"The Hans are one of Seoul's great families," he says hyper-
bolically. "But if you ask me, I find the Hwangs more intrigu-
ing. Why? Great women come from that blood. Haeja has told
you about her Grandmother Hwang?"

"A little," I confess. "I'm afraid she's not very fond of her.
Her great love is Grandma Oh."

"Of course, everyone loves Kao-hai-dong Halmoni," he
says. "But you should get your wife to tell you about Grandma
Hwang. I think she could have been the president of Korea."

"Haeja calls her the Tiger Lady," I say.

"She was a Tiger Lady," admits Uncle Mo. "In a country
where women are often second-class citizens, maybe being a
tiger is a very intelligent disguise. Look at Mrs. Han and her
sisters. They are esteemed women of Korea. Why? Because of
their mother. My own mother always said that Lady Hwang
was one of the great forces of Kyong-Sang Province, and
where would Korea be without people from Kyong-Sang-
Pukdo? The troublemakers like Kim Dae-Jong come from
Cholla. . . ."

"Why do people always say that?" I ask.

"What?"

"About Cholla Province being full of troublemakers."

"Why?" he says, grunting. "Because it is true."

"But so many painters, poets, actors, and musicians come
from Cholla."

"This is also true," Uncle Mo says.

"That makes no sense."

"Cholla is full of great artists and great troublemakers," says
Uncle. "What is the problem with understanding that?"

"Who decided this, and when?" I ask.

"Decided? No one decided. It just happened. Long ago, so long ago that no one remembers when it started. Maybe at the beginning of time and civilization. Since Korea was Korea, Cholla has been trouble, full of troublemakers."

"And artists."

I've noticed that nearly every time I go to a play or dance or music performance in Seoul, the production notes contain biographies of artists from Cholla-do. But the only people I know personally from the province are maids and servants in various households—although it is true that they are invariably colorful and temperamental characters. They seem to have an extra dose of the earthiness I associate with Koreans in general. After all, Korea's Joan of Arc, Yoo Kwan-Soon, was from Cholla; so was the poet Kim Chi-Ha; and the opposition politician, Kim Dae-Jung.

"Troublemakers and artists, troublemaking artists and artistic troublemakers," says Uncle Mo, "that is Cholla Province in a nutshell."

But then I realize that this whole issue of coming from Cholla-do highlights what I had been thinking all along about women in Korea. Without Cholla, I think, Korea would not be what it is, because to an outsider, people from Cholla seem the most Korean of anyone. If Kyong-Sang is Korea's yang, Cholla is its yin, its *um* in Korean.

"There is a simple reason why people from Kyong-Sang are so successful," says my friend. "The most powerful women in Korea—maybe even the world—come from this province. Look at Lady Hwang. She was a feminist long before anyone even knew the word. She was educated, tough, even brilliant. If circumstances had not prevented her, my own mother would have been like Lady Hwang."

Uncle Mo's partisanship was shared in the past by the founder of the Koryo dynasty. Wang Kong preferred Silla women to any other, and Kyong-Sang is a province right in the heart of old Silla. And if I need a historical precedent for Uncle Mo's Kyong-Sang attitude toward Cholla, I find it in ancient Korea, when it was divided into three kingdoms. Koguryo ruled the northern part of the peninsula and into Manchuria; Paekche dominated the southwest, where Cholla is now located; and Silla was a kingdom in the southeast, the present location of Kyongsang Province. During the seventh century Queens Sondok and Chindok led the Silla kingdom during prosperous periods when Korea enjoyed parity with China. Sondok manipulated Paekche into war with Koguryo. Once Paekche defeated Koguryo, Sondok brought in the Chinese to defeat Paekche, then expelled the Chinese but kept their arts and structure of government, unifying the country. By the end of Silla, Queen Chinsong was castigated for bankrupting the court and for her immorality (she had openly taken a lover). Shortly after her reign, the general Wang Kong began the Koryo dynasty. His advice for prosperity? "Marry Silla women," he said, and took his own advice to heart, marrying twenty-six of them in all. But if records from this time are any indication, the Koryo period was even more liberal toward women than Silla was, mainly because of Buddhism's influence.

When the waitress walks by with the pastry cart, Uncle Mo eyes her very intently, and the girl seems to evaporate under his stare. He motions for her to pour us more coffee, even though I protest that I've had enough.

"Pour," he says, and when she does, I see that her hand is shaking. As she walks away he stares at her as though she were a piece of meat. Then he turns back to me and picks up our conversation.

"Even in the old legends about Korea, women had subtle, powerful roles. A princess gets her foolish husband the best horse, thus making him a great warrior. A mother pierces a horse's tongue, making the animal wither, acquires the horse for her son, then nurses the animal back to health, whereupon her son escapes his persecutors, then goes on to become a great horseman and warrior. Eventually he becomes King Tong-myong. Yu the soldier is summoned to the frontier, his wife Kim Si accompanying him; during the night, a tiger captures her husband, but she strikes the beast with her fists, and the tiger gives up her man. Kim Si curses the tiger so badly that the big cat skulks off with its tail between its legs."

He sips his coffee, pinky extended.

"Ah, but I bore you," says Uncle Mo. "You are a writer and know all of this already."

"No," I answer, "this is news to me."

"If you are going to write about Korea," he says, "forget about the men. The women are the real story because everything about them is so subtle, nothing is what it appears to be. Listen to what I am telling you, Michael, if you are going to write about Korea, be sure that you write about the women. Haeja had her differences with her late grandmother, but I tell you it was women like Lady Hwang that made us so tough."

He sips his coffee, then bites into a soft roll. His face goes vacant, then he catches sight of the three rouged college girls across the room. When his eyes engage theirs, they turn their eyes downward shyly. He laughs.

"I love women," says Uncle. "They are . . . life itself." He bites wildly into his roll. "Of course, I am what you might call a feminist," he says, grinning, "and yet it is difficult for me to act like anything but a man in public."

"A tiger never eats another animal with stripes," I say, and he looks puzzled, then he brightens.

"A man admires tigers," says Uncle Mo, grinning from ear to ear. "But he falls in love with a fox."

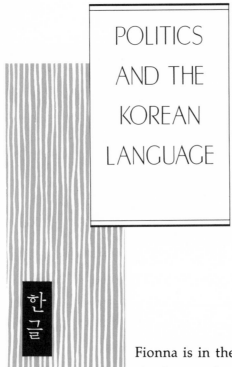

POLITICS AND THE KOREAN LANGUAGE

한글

Fionna is in the habit of calling me Michael instead of father or daddy, and it creates problems in Korea, where first names are almost never used except with younger people. Instead, everyone is referred to by some kind of title: Big Brother *(Hyung-nim)*, Big Sister *(Unni)*, Mother, Father *(Umma, Appa)*. Old people, even when not related to the speaker, are called Grandma and Grandpa; men and women on the street are referred to as Uncle and Aunt.

Because my wife and daughter call me Michael, other people in the household have come to think that this is a kind of honorific, so that even though Koreans seldom use first names, nearly everyone here calls me Michael. But there is a politics to names in Korea, going back to the Confucian notion of right relationships. One morning Haeja referred to the president of Korea in an acceptable American way, using only his last name, Park, and Mrs. Han berated her daughter for a lack of respect.

We know ourselves not so much by our given names, but by our family names and by our titles in relation to those above and below us. To the Hans, I am a son-in-law, and so they may call me Michael, but for me to call them by their given names, Song-Hee and Sae-Hoon, would be an incredible indiscretion. Likewise, husband and wife rarely use their given names, but call each other *Yabo*. To a third party, one of them will refer to his or her mate not as *Yabo* but as *Tong-shin*. Interestingly, *yabo* is a derogatory word for Koreans in Hawaii.

Hae-Soon may call her younger sister Haeja, but Haeja never refers to her older sister by anything other than *Unni*. I may call Haeja's younger brothers by their first names, but they must call me *Hyung-nim*, a title signified by one of the most delightful Chinese characters imaginable, a giant mouth with a set of legs.

"Si" is often added to a last name to make it Mr., Mrs., or Ms, as in Kim-si, Oh-si, Han-si. *Sonsaeng*, Teacher, is an honorific given to educators, but also to anyone who has knowledge or skill of a specialized sort. Thus, a fortune-teller might be called Sonsaeng Ahn. *Sajang* is a title used frequently downtown, as it means "President," and even the smallest business has its sajang-nim. *Jang-goon*, General, is given to the highest military office, but it is used humorously, too. Nicknames proliferate in Korea, and hyperbolic names often get prefixed with the title general. Thus there is the Beer-Belly General, Sleepy General, Piggy General, the Love General, and my favorite, *Dong-jang-goon*, the Shit General, a title given to the man who cleans out the chamber pots from the underside of the old-fashioned houses in the morning, placing the pots on a wooden cart. Mr. Lee once referred to me as a Word General.

Privately, I try to explain to my daughter that it might be better if she calls me Dad or Pop, so her relatives don't get the wrong idea and think her disrespectful, one who does not know the right relationships.

"Has your mother told you about Hong Kiltong, Korea's Robin Hood?" I ask in anticipation of the bedtime story.

"No, Michael," she answers.

"Good," I say, "because this is a story about a man who wanted to call his father 'Father,' but was not able to. His name was Hong Kiltong, and his father was Minister Hong, the head of personnel for the king."

"Which king?" she asks.

"It doesn't matter which king," I say.

"It does," she answers.

It is difficult to resist the requests of a precocious two-year-old, tucked into bed with the covers up to her chin, her big Korean head poking out, her giant dark eyes begging for a story.

"All right," I say. "It was King Sejong, the king who invented the Korean alphabet, the king who lived in the palace at the bottom of the hill."

"That was his home?"

"Every bit of it, and more," I say. "And Mr. Hong was his minister."

"Hong Kiltong's father?"

"Yes," I say, "only he wasn't allowed to call his father 'Father.'"

"Why not?"

"Minister Hong had two sons, In-Hyong and Kiltong, but only the first was allowed to call him father. The other son, Kiltong, was illegitimate."

142

"What's *illegitimate* mean?" It crosses my mind that *Goodnight, Moon* or *Runaway Bunny* might make a better bedtime story.

"It's like he was a stepson or something," I say.

"Like Cinderella?"

"Yes, Hong Kiltong's life was a little like Cinderella's."

"But I thought Hong Kiltong was like Robin Hood."

"His life was like Cinderella's because he was a stepson, sort of, but the things he did were like Robin Hood."

"Stealing from the rich and giving to the poor," she says, "and he wore a glass slipper and his carriage turned into a pumpkin at midnight."

"Only he didn't have a glass slipper or a carriage that turned into a pumpkin," I answer. "I mean, his father treated him badly like Cinderella's stepmother did." I get back to the story.

"It happened that Minister Hong had a dream of thunderbolts and dragons, a good omen if you want to have a child."

As the story goes, Minister Hong was horny and he went to see his wife in her bedchamber, wishing to make love, but his wife refused him. As he walked the halls of his home, he found one of the maids, the young and beautiful Ch'unsom. I don't know how to explain this to Fionna, and I skip ahead in my mind, trying to figure how to make the story more appropriate for a small girl.

"His father was Minister Hong," I say, "but his mother was a maid, and he was a beautiful, brilliant child. Even though he was a child of a servant, whenever he was exposed to learning, Kiltong did very well. It was said that he only had to be told one thing to learn one hundred.

"There was a time when the minister delighted in the company of his precocious son, but after Kiltong turned eight years old, the father refused to let the boy call him 'Father,' or to let the boy refer to the minister's other son as 'Brother.'

"In the full moon of the ninth month, the boy got to thinking. He knew that he could not model his life on the right relationships because he was the son of his father and yet was not allowed to say he was the son of his father, nor to call him that. He had a brother, too, but was not allowed to call his brother 'Brother.' Yet he was permitted to refer to his mother as 'Mother.' He wondered, should he meet the king, if he would be allowed to call him King, or would he have to refer to him as something else. Or, when he made friends, whether he would be able to call them 'Friend.' If he married, would he call his wife 'Wife' and his children, 'Son' and 'Daughter.' So because he was not able to model his life after Confucius and Mencius, the two great Chinese philosophers whom all Koreans emulated, Kiltong decided to leave home and make his own fortune—you see, in Korea it is important to use the proper relationships in referring to your family members.

"Anyhow, Kiltong went out into the world by himself, and he met highwaymen and outcasts in his travels, and like Robin Hood, he formed a band of do-good outlaws, who stole from the rich and gave to the poor, and lived with great respect for one another. And soon his name became known everywhere. He was the only man who could help ordinary people against wealthy landowners and government officials. . . ." But when I pause I see that Fionna is asleep, and so I tiptoe out of the study and into the kitchen where several members of the family as well as a few of the ajima, their work finished for the day, are watching television. The low table has been moved aside after the meal. Those watching the show sit on the floor or on pillows, resting their backs against the wall.

I have come in in the middle of a historic soap opera about King Sejong, who created Hangul, the Korean alphabet, in the mid-fifteenth century. In this particular scene, the king is conferring with Ch'oe Malli, one of his nobles, about his scholarly work. It seems that Ch'oe Malli objects to the alphabet which he refers to as *un moon,* "vulgar sounds." The actor playing the noble spits out the phrase with great disdain. He says, "Only barbarians have their own alphabets. Matters of the barbarians are not worth our time discussing."

I like Sejong's plain answer: "The people need an alphabet."

Ch'oe bows obsequiously.

"Change the barbarians using Chinese ways. We have never heard of changing toward barbarousness."

Chong, a court scholar, steps forward: "We are prepared to print any book there is and all men will have the means of study."

"Nonsense," says Ch'oe. Chong tells him that literature will increase and grow, and religion will flourish on the Earth. "Heresy" and "barbaric vulgarities," says Ch'oe.

King Sejong steps forward. "In our Eastern Sector, ceremonials, music, and literature are comparable to those of China, but our local speech is not the same. Students of books are troubled by the difficulty of understanding the meaning of Chinese characters. Legal texts are nearly unreadable. We borrowed Chinese characters to write our native tongue, but this writing is not a true native expression. Some of these Chinese sounds grate on the ear, others stop you completely when you try to make them Korean." Soon enough the dialogue ceases, and as is typical of these historic soap operas on Korean television, well choreographed slow-motion scenes of martial arts between myriad forces fill the picture tube.

Up until the time of Sejong, Koreans had their own spoken language, but no written one. Instead, they used Chinese characters, transposing them into Korean by a system of clerical writing known as *idu*. More than half of the vocabulary in Korean is derived from Chinese, too, though grammar and some pronunciations are quite different. Over the centuries, the gap between Korean as it was spoken and as it was written with Chinese characters widened until only educated Korean nobles and Buddhist monks were able to read the written language.

The earliest surviving use of Hangul is in an encomium to the Yi family, founders of the dynasty, entitled *Songs of the Dragons*. Shortly thereafter, Sejong encouraged the Buddhist monks to use the phonetic alphabet for their scriptures, because the nobles continued to prefer Chinese, no doubt out of snobbery and habit, and Hangul was on its way to becoming a minority script, employed by the out-of-favor Buddhists and the vernacular writers. One of the first to put the new script to common use was Ho Kyun, the son of an Yi minister, and the brother of the well-known poet Nonsorhon, who worked in *kasa*—a lyrical form inspired by contemporary songs. Along with folk dramas, p'ansori, and the popular fictions like Ho Kyun's, the Korean alphabet as a literary medium was used by poets working in kasa and a long-limbed, three-line form known as *sijo*. The court poets continued to use Chinese.

Ho's story in Hangul form was inspired by a Chinese fable, but colored to Korean tastes. Although it was a popular entertainment, it was also a political attack on neo-Confucian values, especially the treatment of illegitimate children. Though his father was a well-known government official, Ho Kyun's friends were all, in fact, illegitimate sons, and eventually he would be executed along with them for plotting against the government.

Ho Kyun also wrote the story about Hong Kiltong that I told

Fionna—perhaps the first example of Hangul's use in prose fiction.

Haeja, Fionna, and I buy tickets at a booth near the palace wall, then enter the gardens through a prospect of lace-bark pines and paulownia trees. Fionna wants to see the swans on the pond near Kyung-ho-ru Pavilion and the pretty little bridge that crosses the lotus pond at Kyangwon-jong. Then she wants to stop for *cider*—a soda like 7-Up—at the stand near the National Museum.

She pulls on my pant leg.

"Ice cream," she says.

"Not now," I say, "later."

"Don't be mean," Haeja says.

I want to visit the scholar's pavilion where the alphabet was invented.

"They don't have ice cream here," I say. Fionna gives me a look of utter disbelief—for the life of her she can't understand how a palace could be a palace if there's no ice cream.

After a few minutes of walking around, both Haeja and Fionna are hot and tired.

"You go to your sister's," I tell Haeja. "I'll visit the scholar's pavilion by myself and meet you afterward." Usually Haeja doesn't like us to drift apart outside the house; she remembers all too well the day when I got lost in Nadaemun Market. But it is so hot, and her sister's house is so near, that she agrees. Alone, I wander over to a set of tiny pavilions behind the throne room of the palace.

Korea must be the only country in the world that has a national holiday for its alphabet. The pavilion, however, turns out to be a modest structure painted a barnyard red, no bigger

147

than a bungalow. Yet Korea might not be Korea, I think, if not for these events that took place here, because the yangban were content to keep Chinese as the medium of literary expression in the court, employing it perhaps as White Russians used French, as a way to show class and culture. A commoner, even a peasant, might know how to read and write Hangul script, but it was doubtful he would be able to use Chinese characters.

Perhaps that's why I associate the invention of the Korean alphabet with a kind of *goong hop*—that unnameable ingredient that must exist between two people before they can get married. In King Sejong's case, the *goong hop* was between himself and his times. Korea, like China, had been laid seige to by the Mongols, but Kublai Khan's reign had ended around the time that Sejong's ancestors had founded the Yi dynasty. By the time of Sejong's own rule, a generation or two later, the Korean world was ripe for initiative. Japan was relatively dormant, and no European besides Marco Polo had yet found a route to the Far East. Yet the times preceding and following Sejong's reign were anything but idyllic.

Though his father had been a harsh ruler and some of his relatives were barbaric and downright murderous, Sejong was a lucky combination of intelligence and firmness, sensitivity and strength. He was also a born leader; the Will of Heaven reflected benignly on him.

His grandfather had founded a dynasty but died without laying out a clear line of succession among his sons. The brothers went to killing each other until Sejong's father manipulated events, allowing one to succeed—but only if he would abdicate after a short while and give the crown to Sejong's father. By the time that Sejong came to power, the new dynasty was firmly established, and Seoul had become the capital of the nation. Moveable type was already in use, years before Gutenberg's "invention." After his death, another round of bloody internecine strife followed.

Sejong had what later, in the West, would be called a Renaissance temperament: like Leonardo Da Vinci, he excelled at many pursuits, both artistic and practical. This combination was a kind of human perfection to the neo-Confucianists of his time. His language project was but one of many intellectual activities. A tinkerer, Sejong wanted to know more about Chinese armillary clocks and water systems; he marveled at the ducts and flues under the palace buildings, which provided heat to the ondol floors. Sometimes admiringly, sometimes critically, it was said that his best friends were books. Korea had not experienced a rule by enlightenment like his since the Silla dynasty seven centuries earlier.

Wandering around the tiny pavilion I can almost see Sejong and his scholars sitting cross-legged at low tables, their writerly accoutrements spare and essential. There would be a scholar's lamp, weasel-tail brushes, rice paper, bookshelves of scholarly tomes stacked vertically. One scribe might have an Indian inkstone: he would grind it on the flat black surface of a writing box, then mix the powder with water for the proper consistency.

Hangul is based on three simple elements: a dot represents Heaven; a horizontal line for the Earth; and a vertical one for Man. Each of the twenty-eight letters of the alphabet are formed from these three elements.

The Middle Kingdom, China, had been the center of the universe for centuries on centuries. Its language was the medium of the Korean court; its thought and ideas were the currency of educated Korean men; and its art and culture were the art and culture of Korea as well. Sejong's task was to bring scholarly endeavor within the scope of this system; but he also had to mask the nationalism of this enterprise. By employing Chinese cosmology in the structure of the Korean alphabet, he assuaged the conservatism of his nobles at the court in Seoul, who so doggedly emulated everything Chinese. Politically, Sejong was a bit like Won Hyo, the great wandering monk of Silla dynasty who introduced Buddhism to the common people. Setting out from the Diamond Mountains to make a pilgrimage to China, Won Hyo discovered that he did not have to go to China, since China was already in his mind.

With the invention of the Korean alphabet, not only did kings and commoners share a written language, but, for the first time, the nation could begin to wipe out illiteracy. (Today, Korea is one of the few countries in which nearly everyone reads and writes.) The alphabet, being phonetic, also allowed people with a knowledge of Chinese characters to render their sounds into Korean. With the alphabet, Korea began to outgrow its status as an outpost dependency of China.

King Sejong's last political act was to entrust the new alphabet to the Buddhist monks, who, with the ascendancy of neo-Confucian ideas, had fallen out of favor. The court was filled with practical scholars, but the monasteries held an untapped reservoir of intellectual talent, a powerless concatenation of holy men, scribes, and scholars. Sejong informed the monks that the new alphabet would be a great vehicle for promoting Buddhist texts among the common people, who had no way of learning Chinese characters. In essence, Sejong bequeathed the new alphabet to a band of outlaw scholars, as a way of getting around the conservatism of the court. It is quite possible that Hangul would have fallen into disuse after Sejong's demise if not for the monks, who vigorously translated Buddhist works into Hangul.

From the mid-fifteenth century until the end of World War II, Korean continued to have two forms of literary expression: the Chinese preferred by the nobility, and Hangul used by popular storytellers like Ho Kyun and poets like his sister, Nonsorhon, and also by the common people, the monks, and those mysterious beauties, the kisaeng.

Hangul retained this acceptance until Japan annexed the peninsula in this century and outlawed it. Suddenly, merely to write a poem in Korean became an incredible political act. Traces of this are still evident: Koreans of the Hans' generation are often better able to read and write Japanese than Korean. From 1910 until the end of World War II, the Korean language was practiced clandestinely, usually in the home. During the Second World War, Japanese determination to crush native Korean expression went so far as to make Koreans take Japanese names. But the Japanese did not succeed in these attempts, and by the end of the war the use and promulgation of Hangul became a nationalistic imperative, the pride of all Koreans. Hangul's inherent political implications, though, aren't just nationalistic, for even today the most dangerous profession a young Korean can aspire to is a writer. Sejong's great democratic invention has the bite of a sword when it is wielded in the realm of a military government.

Grandma Oh greets me at the door of the Lees' house, and I go into the courtyard, up the steps, and take off my shoes before entering the living room. One maid brings me a cold bottle of "cider," while another sets down a plate of sliced watermelon. The children play in the side room while the sisters and their grandmother talk. Mr. Han's son Byung-Su comes out of his room to say hello, but quickly excuses himself because he is preparing for a medical exam at school. Mr.

Lee is at work, probably not expected to return until late in the evening. It is too soon to go back home. The heat and humidity have wiped me out, and I tell Haeja that I'd like to lie down.

Hae-Soon shows me a tiny bedroom, a cool space no bigger than a berth on a train. The mat laid out on the floor and the small table next to it take up most of the room, and less than a foot of space remains once I stretch out. I slide the rice paper door shut, and open a rice paper window that looks out over the tiniest of courtyards, where a miniature pine thrives. As I drift off I hear birdsong and, opening an eye, I see a little sparrow giving itself a dirt bath. As soon as I fall asleep, I am visited by an old Chinese philosopher. In front of me appear yarrow stalks and a copy of *The Book of Changes*.

"Yang," he says, "is male, Heaven. It is light, active, warm, dry. Remember this." He draws on a long pipe. "Yin," he continues, "is female, the Earth. It is passive, cold, dark, moist. Think of what I am saying." But he doesn't give me time to think about anything.

"Listen carefully to what I am saying," he instructs me. "You are married to the second daughter, Li, the Changing. She is the giver of light and her image is Fire. Her elder sister is Sun, the Gentle. Remember what I am telling you. Her attribute is penetration. *Unni* is her title. She penetrates with her gaze." Then the ancient philosopher gets weird on me: he pulls a long-necked bottle of Budweiser from a fold in his robes, pops the cap, and kicks back a wad of suds. "She sees through everyone's bullshit," he says, smacking his lips. As quickly as that, though, he is gone, and the room is transformed again.

When I come to, sweaty, my mouth cruddy, my ears filled with ringing, I hear the children shouting in the courtyard. They sing a song about a rabbit, *Santoki-toki-ya*. The bird has flown the coop, and already it is evening. Awakening unexpectedly in this tiny traditional room, in this tiny traditional house, I realize that this is how most people wake in Seoul. I get up, slide open the door and find myself in the narrow hallway, then slide open another door, step down, put on my shoes, and come into the courtyard.

At the top of the hill, the rooster crows, letting us know we are in the vicinity of Samchung-dong. A magpie calls, a dog barks. It occurs to me—all these creatures speak Korean. The neighborhood dogs bark as we pass by the opened doors of tiny houses on the hillside: they don't say *Woof! Woof!,* they say *Mung! Mung! Mung!*

"Now I shall explain the theory behind Heaven, Earth, Man, and the creation of Hangul, the Korean alphabet," the lecturer says.

"The throat is deep and moist," he says, then pauses to drink a glass of water. "Like water," says the man, holding up his glass, "like winter." I look at my watch and think how slow time can be. "Though empty and transparent," he goes on, "it flows, it is deep and moist." From the podium, I hear words like "metal," "incisor," "autumn," but I can no longer make sense of what he is saying.

He holds a piece of paper in his hand. "Consider the time in which Sejong lived, and you will see that it was not luck so much as fortune, the Will of Heaven, that allowed for this possibility of the new alphabet," I hear him as I drift off.

When I awake, the lecturer is quoting from Sejong's scholarly work on the language project, entitled *Hunmin chong'um* (The Correct Sounds for the Instruction of the People). "The sounds of our country's language are different from those of the Middle Kingdom, they do not run together with the sounds of characters. Therefore, among the ignorant people, there have been many who, having something they want to put into words, have in the end been unable to express their feelings. I have been distressed by this, and have newly designed twenty-eight letters, which I wish to have everyone practice at their ease and make convenient for their daily use."

He goes on to explain that sounds like "oh, "ah," "ya," and "yo" are situated above and on the outside of the mouth.

"This is because, emerging from Heaven, they are yang, the masculine." He writes the symbols in Korean and their corresponding sounds in English on a chalkboard:

┤ oh

├ ah

┝ ya

╡ yo

"Sounds like 'oo,' the softer 'oh,' 'yoo,' and the softer 'yoh' are situated below and on the inside of the mouth. This is because, emerging from Earth, they are Um, what some call Yin, the feminine." He returns to the board and writes the Earth sounds in Korean with their English counterparts.

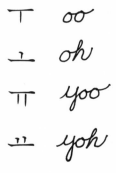

┬ oo

⊥ oh

╥ yoo

⊥⊥ yoh

"It should be remembered," he continues, "that Heaven and Earth complete the Myriad Things, but it is Man who supports and perfects these materials. Man is entrusted with the pattern." He illustrates his point.

heaven   earth   man

When women speak Korean, their voices are like poetry, their mouths full of lilting vowels, turning the simplest words and conversations into Italian arias. Some people say that Korean is an Altaic language, related to Hungarian and Finnish. Underscoring their utterances I hear gypsy violins, the lovely, earthy anarchy of the farmers' bands, the reedy horns like late John Coltrane.

In the mouths of men, Korean is grittier—the speech of horsemen, nomads, mountain men. Equally of the Earth, the sounds are glutinous like thick rice, like thick and stringy roots or grain alcohol. Yet their speech is also heavenly, even though it comes from the balls, inflecting around the kneecaps, full of sweat and agriculture and, nowadays, industrial soot. The Korean of men has the poetry of the jackhammer.

The lecturer has been speaking about the patterns in the Korean alphabet, and an American speaks up to say that he doesn't understand. A woman sitting one row ahead of me and two seats over raises her hand. She looks different from anyone I've seen in Seoul—taller than most Korean women, and she wears glasses and a man's fedora—like someone I might run into at a poetry reading in Manhattan. She has on deep red lipstick, accentuating her mouth, a silk blouse with several buttons undone, and a string of pearls around her neck, and her long hair is an intense black. She smokes, and it occurs to me that she may be the first Korean women I've seen with a cigarette in public. She stands.

"Breath and syllable have a nature as immutable as the patterns in jade, the grain of wood, the lifeline in the palm of a hand, the vein of pink marble, the gristle in meat, the red of a pepper, the hoot of an owl, the crow of a cock, the sneeze from a cold, the warmth from the sun, the rain in clouds. It is like making an ax from an ax handle. The pattern is never very far. Heaven, Earth, *Human.* Dot, vertical, horizontal. The sounds for appeasing spirits. The invention of the alphabet. Patterns." She sits down flushed, her chest heaving.

Without even the slightest acknowledgment of this extraordinary remark, the lecturer calls on another person.

"That was great," I whisper.

"Thank you," she replies, and lights another cigarette, her hand shaking. I tap her on the shoulder and whisper, "Can it really be translated 'human' instead of 'man'? I mean, is that what it's saying, human instead of man?"

It's a beautiful fall day turning into evening, and I am back in New York. I have just come from a lecture by a Korean professor at Columbia University, a public talk on the Korean language. For all intents and purposes, it could have been the same lecture I heard in Seoul a year or two earlier. The leaves are on the ground, and a chill drifts through the evening air. The sky is cloudless and unpolluted, the light slants off the Hudson, reddish yellow, brilliant. In a few days, children will be out trick-or-treating. Tonight, I have no plans beyond dinner and reading.

When I walk in the door, Haeja asks. "Did you hear?"

"Hear what," I say, taking off my jacket, slipping off my shoes.

Haeja tells me that after nearly two decades of complete power President Park—the former teacher and general, the martinet with an "economic miracle" and prisons for dissenters, the man from Kyong-Sang Province who declared martial law, the little dictator with an iron will, who called his military state a democracy, that fierce anti-Communist "strongman"— is dead. Assassinated, she says, by one of his own men. It's difficult to know whether to jump for joy or sit down and worry. The politics of Korea are like that.

"My sister called a while ago from Seoul," says Haeja. "The head of Korean Central Intelligence did it. They had an argument over the student demonstrations and what to do, and the director shot him dead."

"Park was assassinated," I repeat, but I still don't really believe it.

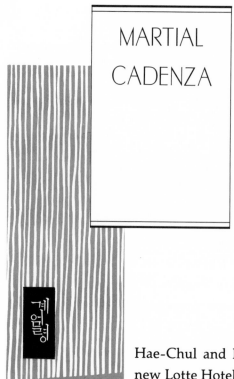

MARTIAL CADENZA

계열령

Hae-Chul and I sit in the lobby of the new Lotte Hotel in the center of the city. We are in a lounge, looking out a gigantic picture window into a frozen waterfall, snow everywhere. The room is cavernous, full of mirrors, potted palms, sleek escalators, walls of pale marble, brass fixtures. Myong-dong is the shopping district of Seoul, the so-called Fifth Avenue, but Lotte is Fifth Avenue at one venue with its department store, luxury hotel, underground arcades, rooftop restaurants, and various malls with Korean fast-food noodle shops, bulgoki and kalbi houses, and bee-bim-bop shops serving vegetables, rice, and slivers of meat with hot sauce in steaming crocks. I am told that the Lotte Corporation began with a Japanese-Korean businessman making cookies, selling soda and chewing gum, and that the name comes from Lotte Lenya, the executive's favorite

158

singer. Yet this is the last place on Earth I would expect to hear Kurt Weill and Bertolt Brecht's *Threepenny Opera*.

On my last visit to Seoul, Hae-Chul was still working in Europe, so this is a time for us to get to know each other; we've only met twice briefly, in New York. We sip whiskies as waitresses in colorful traditional dress breeze past with trays of drinks for tables of American and Korean businessmen. Mr. Lee and Byung-Jeen are to meet us later for dinner at one of the new rooftop restaurants.

This visit we are staying in Hae-Chul's new house just south of the Han residence, and since my arrival I have peppered him with questions about the events of the last year in Korea.

"The assassination must have taken place right on the other side of your fence," I say.

"No, no," Hae-Chul answers. "We live on the southeast side of the Blue House grounds. The assassination was outside the northwest perimeter, maybe a mile away."

"Out on that road that leads to the observatory overlooking Seoul?"

"More or less," says Hae-Chul as he sips his whiskey. "But why are you still so interested in the assassination?"

The assassination took place over a year ago, but I still think about it constantly, piecing together the incident from accounts I've seen in various newspapers and magazines and on television. I can't rid myself of an interest in that historical evening, and I go over the details I have accumulated as if they were the accretions from a good mystery or thriller.

The head of the Korean Central Intelligence, Kim Jae-Kyu, had invited President Park, his chief of staff, Cha Chi-Chol, and Mr. Kim, the Presidential Secretary, to a Company safehouse on the northwest border of the Blue House for an evening of eating, drinking, and partying. As the evening progressed, J.K. argued with Mr. Cha, the bitter words about politics and personal animosity. Finally, J.K. killed Cha, the Presidential Secretary, and President Park.

Still, Hae-Chul was right; the assassination was history, almost from another time, when Korea was ruled for two decades by a general turned politician. The events that followed the assassination now seem more affecting and disquieting than the murder itself. After the assassination, people in the southern provinces demanded an open election, an end to military government, a democratic reform. First the riot police were sent, but then General Chun, who assumed power when martial law was declared right after the assassination, released the garrison to quell the insurrection in the city of Kwangju in Cholla Province. The government claimed that a few hundred rioters were killed; others said that thousands of innocent civilians were slaughtered. In theory, the American military was in charge of these particular Korean troops, but they did nothing to stop the bloodshed. More demonstrations followed, and finally martial law was enacted and a curfew imposed on the major cities. Now, a year after the assassination of Park Chung-Hee, his protege General Chun is in charge of the government. Like his precedessor, he is from Kyong-Sang Province.

A lot of people thought I was crazy coming to Seoul while it was still under martial law. Oddly, I felt no uneasiness about coming and, sitting here in the hotel lobby, I still felt no fear, no uneasiness. But I notice I'm drinking more than usual, that the talkative, often ebullient, wonderfully humorous Hae-Chul is strangely quiet—not morose exactly, but not his cheerful self. It's almost as if everything we say is being monitored and Hae-Chul is wary of making a gaffe.

Of course, it is difficult to imagine any of these events while sitting in the lobby of a hotel named for Lotte Lenya. A cancerous inflation, political disaffections, and personal grievances pale in the unreal comfort and luxury of this plush lobby. Besides, I am sitting with Hae-Chul, the ultimate optimist, a man who believes that a good sense of humor, hard work, and intelligence will transform any dire situation into a winning cause. To Hae-Chul, anything Korean is inherently dramatic, even sad, but the outcome is always upbeat and positive; he believes in the infinite potential of all things.

If Korea were to send its representative man of the last quarter of this century into distant space in search of other worlds, I often think their ideal astronaut would be someone like Hae-Chul. Neither tall nor short, he is incredibly broad-shouldered, thick-necked, and his suit jacket can't hide his massive biceps. But his most telling quality is his sense of humor, which would sustain him during a long ordeal of flight to the distant place beyond the Milky Way to which Koreans hearken when romantically—or is it amorously?—inclined. Though he's a businessman—he was educated at Kyongghi High School and attended Seoul National University—I sense more whimsy and pleasure than pragmatism and functionality in him. He is a family man but he has many friends outside the family—in fact, all over the world—with whom he loves to eat, drink, and spend time. Besides being garrulous, Hae-Chul is a thoughtful and philosophical man. Before anything else, he's a music lover; he surrounds himself with it—Mozart to Elvis—in his house, in the car, walking on the street, sitting in the lobby of the hotel. The Music of the Spheres would no doubt intrigue him.

As we sit in the Lotte Hotel lobby, I muse over the idea of Hae-Chul in space. When I tell him what I've been thinking, his eyes light up, but he dismisses it. "They would need some-one with a more scientific background than my own."

"If that's the only thing stopping you," I say, "then I'm sure you'll be the one."

"But this ideal Korean who ventures into space," he muses, "I think he should be a good golfer, too."

"That's you, too," I laugh.

"Not quite," he admits. "My drive is long, but I'm prone to slicing the ball."

"Imagine a space alien being offered garlic and kim-chee for the first time."

"Oh, I'm sure the aliens would like it," he deadpans. Our fanciful digression falls away, and I return to the earlier sub-ject—having thoroughly confused any nearby spies.

"Something different is in the air," I say.

"Different from what?"

"From the last time I was here."

"A new luxury hotel," he says, smiling.

"I mean outside on the street."

Hae-Chul gives me the look of a businessman listening skeptically to a writer with an overactive imagination. "The economy is doing quite well." He sips longer and more pen-sively at his whiskey. "Everyone in the family is doing well. What more can one ask for?"

But he knows what I mean; it is just that some things are best understood silently, between the lapses in the conversation. He also knows that I won't swallow the party line.

"One military government has been replaced by another one," I finally say.

"True," he nods.

"Kwangju," I whisper.

That word alone makes Hae-Chul blanch, turn inward, no longer jocular. He nods his head slowly, then nods it more vigorously. "Yes, yes," he says, absentmindely motioning to one of the waitresses. "Let's go eat."

"L'addition," he says, scribbling with his hand in the air on an imaginary tally sheet.

We take one of the sleek new escalators up several flights, then switch to an elevator, and although we are a few minutes early, Mr. Lee and Byung-Jeen are already waiting outside the restaurant at the top of the hotel. It advertises itself as French, but really it is Korean—the only difference between it and a traditional *shik-dahng* is the tremendous amount of cream in which the meat and vegetables are soaked. But there are also plates of kim-chee and familiar roots, peppery cucumbers, and, of course, lots of garlic on everything.

It is still early in the evening and a buffet has been laid out. The three men heap their plates with creamy chicken, creamy vegetables, creamy soup, creamy oysters, and take a bottle of California white wine to their table. I opt for smoked salmon. After nearly seven years of marriage, I know that dairy products and Koreans don't mix. Because that is so, I also know that otherwise admirable Korean chefs don't have the slightest clue about something as alien as cream. They do know about fish, though, and the salmon looks and tastes quite fresh.

We sit down at an overly large, formal table in the center of the restaurant. It's crowded with tiny pieces of china, blindingly polished silverware, crystal goblets for wine and water, and napkins and a table cloth as white as the new snow on the ground outside.

"To your new president," Hae-Chul salutes me.

"Yes, yes, to your new president," Mr. Lee agrees, raising his glass.

"Well, I didn't vote for him," I say.

"He will be good for Korea," declares Hae-Chul.

Perhaps, I think, but will he be good for America? "To your new president, too." I raise my glass in salute, but no one raises a glass with me. Instead, the three men dig into their various creams.

When I look around the big restaurant, I notice that we are almost the only customers. Outside, snow is falling. Across the room, I see four musicians, two men and two women, setting up. They tune up, then dive into a Mozart quartet with incredible gusto and musicianship. I had forgotten how music-crazy all Koreans are, not just my brother-in-law Hae-Chul. It is impossible to be anywhere in Seoul without hearing some kind of music, even if it is only a delivery man humming a commercial jingle.

"Have some French cuisine," Hae-Chul prods me, holding up his half-empty plate.

"I prefer the smoked salmon," I answer. "It reminds me of Zabar's in New York."

"Ah, ah, Zabar's," Mr. Lee says. "That is appa's favorite place in New York."

Now our table is surrounded by seven or eight waiters with nothing to do but ask us how we like our food. The quartet joins them, moving around the circular table like a pack of gypsies in tuxedos and evening gowns. Outside, Seoul is in twilight—our only accommodation to martial law is dining earlier than usual in order to have a full evening on the town before curfew.

When we finish the meal, Byung-Jeen complains of a stomachache from the creamy sauces; Mr. Lee says he must go

shopping for Christmas presents for his children in Myong-
dong. Hae-Chul and I wander off together in search of nightlife.

It is extremely cold and dry outside, the snow has ended, and
the night air invigorating. The streets are strangely empty,
considering that Seoul is one of the most populous cities in the
world. I think about all the variations on the word "white" in
the Korean language. There is *huida;* but there is also *hayat'a,*
a kind of white-white. There is also bone white, death white,
rice paper white, cotton white, even creamy sauce white. *Saep-
poyat'a* is a good way to describe both the cream sauces in the
restaurants and the old snow on the ground. And the newly
fallen snow is more of a *hoyomologot'a,* brand-new white. As the
whiteness of the neon signs merges with the whiteness of the
snow on the ground, I think of other whites: *huippuyot'a, ppuyot'a,
hoyosurumhada, hayasurumhada, hoyot'a, ppoyat'a, huimolgot'a,* the
whiteness of a doorman's gloves, a baby's teeth, an old
woman's hair, the starched white of pillows and sheets. But
finally it is too cold for walking, so we step into a nightclub
for drinks and entertainment.

Most of the rock groups seem to come from the Philippines,
their songs rendered in a refreshingly broken English. We don't
stay long, and as we are leaving, a Korean magician marches
onto the stage to the sounds of John Phillip Sousa's tubas and
other horns.

The moment we step outside, Hae-Chul's driver pulls up in
a small black Pony sedan and, once inside the car, we speed off
into the night. I have *never* understood how this is synchronized
so well.

Once again the snow falls, blanketing the city. The streets
are empty of pedestrians and cars, and we move quickly from
downtown into the northern part of the city along Sejong-ro.

On both sides of the street are soldiers and tanks, reminding me of photos I saw when I was a boy and the Korean War filled the front pages of newspapers, the Americans slogging through ice, sleet, and snow as they progressed north toward the North Koreans and the Chinese Communists.

"I hope we get back soon," says Hae-Chul from the front seat. "That cream sauce is dancing inside my stomach." To distract himself, he flips a cassette into the machine on the dashboard, and through a panorama of speakers Creedence Clearwater booms out. The night Park Chung-Hee was assassinated just up the road from where we are now, he was serenaded by Shim Soo-Bang, a torch singer; his food was served by Ms. Shin, a popular actress. But when I hear Creedence on the car stereo and I see the tanks and the soldiers on the street, I think of Vietnam, the sound that of helicopter rotors and John Fogarty's bluesy voice growling "Bad Moon Rising."

I look out the window from Hae-Chul's living room to the garden filled with snow, icicles dripping from the fruit trees, the more delicate shrubbery wrapped in burlap. Inside the house, logs crackle in the fireplace, and Hae-Chul picks out "Eleanor Rigby" on the spinet piano in the corner. Haeja sits at the table in the dining room, talking with her grandmother. Fionna sits on one of the couches, looking at a children's picture book while her two-year-old cousin Kyung-Su reclines on the rug, taking the doors off a toy Lamborghini car we brought him from Mi-Guk. The boy's mother sits erect on a couch, staring at a tapestry of Leda and the swan, bought in Brussels, which hangs over the mantelpiece.

Every object in the house reflects Hae-Chul's wife Ok-Hyun's high-flown European tastes—chairs from Paris, couches from England, coffee tables from Italy, tapestries from

Belgium, vases from the Netherlands, and a stereo from West Germany. Two years spent in Europe created this style, and the effect is of somewhere thousands of miles from Korea, and from another era, too. I imagine a parlor in a Chekhov story, the beautiful but somehow doomed gentry awaiting their ultimate decline and the revolution. The only contemporary note is Hae-Chul, boyishly enthusiastic at the piano, picking his way by ear and untrained but deft fingers through "Norwegian Wood," to which he lends his mellifluous tenor.

He calls Haeja from the dining room, and gets her to sing a few Christmas carols on this cold, clear December night. It occurs to me that this is the night the Japanese bombed Pearl Harbor, but there have already been enough layers of irony to the evening, and I refrain from mentioning it. The interior world here changes little, always this loving, familial core. It is outside where everything has deteriorated. Pearl Harbor is irrelevant to the security of this familiar cocoon, the lights from the Hans' living room visible over the garden wall; but it is not irrelevant to what goes on outside on the street, the soldiers and tanks everywhere.

As Haeja sings, the world seems at peace. Cigarettes, alcohol, and motherhood have had little effect on the coloring of her soprano; martial law hasn't dampened its timbre. My thoughts turn from Chekhov to Dickens's happy-ending scenes, the goose in its pot, the fire crackling, the good guys vindicated. Haeja sings, "Come all ye faithful, joyful and triumphant, O come ye, come ye to Bethlehem. . . ."

"Ah, that Haeja has good vocal chords," says Grandma Oh, entering.

She fumbles in the pockets of her hanbok for her cigarettes and lighter, carrying the duck-shaped ashtray that we gave her several years earlier.

"Ok-Hyun-ah," calls Hae-Chul. "Get Halmoni some egg-nog with cognac."

"*Ahni,* no, no," Grandma Oh says, drawing out her words. "The milk makes my stomach sick. Bring me a plate of that spicy summer kim-chee instead."

"You can't eat kim-chee and nothing else, Halmoni." Haeja is concerned about her grandmother's health.

"But she's right about the milk," Haeja says to her brother. "I have the same problem digesting milk products."

"An enzyme deficiency in the stomach," Hae-Chul says. "Most Asians are allergic to lactose."

"And alcohol," his wife Ok-Hyun quips.

"We drink alcohol better than anyone," he responds.

"Then why does your face turn so red at the first sip of alcohol? Why do your eyes get bloodshot and run with tears? How come your skin breaks out in a rash?"

"Only the first drink," Hae-Chul says. "Then my mind and body settle down to enjoy the booze."

"An allergy," his wife says. "Just like you have with lactose. You shouldn't drink milk or alcohol."

"I'll cut out milk," Hae-Chul says, and goes back to the spinet, listening to a song in his head, then picking it out on the keys of the piano. He hums the melody to "Yellow Submarine" as he finds the keys that match his voice.

"He's impossible," Ok-Hyun tells Haeja.

"Leave Hae-Chul alone," says Grandma. "He's a good boy."

"Impossible," repeats his wife, and whispers to Haeja, "He's thirty years old and she spoils him like he was still a little child." Even if Grandma Oh seems as old as the hills, her senses are unusually sensitive and quick at times.

"I heard you, I hear fine," says Halmoni. "I spoil him, of

168

course, but he's my only boy." Then to Hae-Chul: "Play that nice song about Private Kochee by the Peetles." Hae-Chul looks to his wife and sister for help, not sure what Grandma Oh is talking about.

Then Kyung-Su, the boy, pipes in "Sergeant Peppah!"

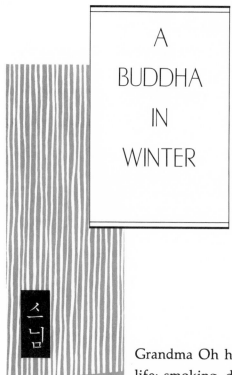

A
BUDDHA
IN
WINTER

Grandma Oh has three pleasures left in life: smoking, drinking, and cursing.

She tokes on her Milky Way cigarette, coughs, takes a slug of whiskey for her aches, mutters, "Fucking bastards, fucking bastards . . ."

The smoking she learned from her husband when she was sixteen years old, several lifetimes ago. The whiskey drinking is new: Mr. Lee and her grandson Hae-Chul had the idea that it would ease her aches and pains. People say that the cursing is second nature to her, her own mode of expression. In Halmoni's mouth, the vernacular becomes a kind of poetry.

Sometime between our last visit to Korea and now, Grandma Oh has moved from the Lees' old house to Hae-Chul's new solar-heated house. With the move, she acquired a new name: now she is called Samchung-dong Halmoni.

Hae-Chul and I lounge on one of the overstuffed sofas in the living room, listening to Elvis Presley on the stereo; Grandma Oh complains about her gums, and everything and nothing in particular.

"Gil-Butts," Hae-Chul says, getting up. He opens a cabinet and removes a bottle of Korean whiskey, Gilbert's. He pours out two fingers each of whiskey for the three of us.

"Kom-Bai!" he says, saluting Grandma Oh.

She drinks, mutters, sighs. She likes maggoli and soju, even *makju,* beer, but this whiskey is strong and makes her head crazy, gets her swearing and cursing, gives her fits. Grandma Oh has always been known for her colorful speech, but in the old days she directed it at specific people or things. Now it is a malediction against living, against having lived too long.

Soon Halmoni goes off with Haeja and the others. Left alone amidst the European furniture, Hae-Chul and I listen to more music—it seems that he owns every record Elvis ever made—and get philosophical.

"Is the country changed?" I ask. Once again Hae-Chul broods at my question.

Grandma Oh storms back into the living room.

"Gil-Butts," Hae-Chul says again. He pours his grandmother another big tumbler. She drinks it off quickly and he pours her another, but she refuses. She curls up in the reading chair, then suddenly jumps up. "Enough," she says, grabbing the bottle and running out of the living room. Minutes later, Hae-Chul goes to retrieve the bottle.

"She always hides it in the same place."

The next morning, I am sitting in the breakfast nook with Haeja eating rolls and drinking coffee when Halmoni shuffles into the kitchen and plops herself down in a corner on the floor.

"Sit at the table with us," Haeja says.

"No."

Halmoni shuns the Western-style chairs around the break-fast table. She prefers to hunch up on the floor in a corner, Korean-style, her ashtray on one side, her cigarettes and lighter on the other.

"Tell me about grandfather," Haeja asks.

"What is there to say?"

"Tell me what he looked like."

"How would I know?" Grandma says. "I was too shy to look at his face."

"I heard he was very handsome," Haeja says, "that he stud-ied Western opera. Is it true he wanted to go off to Europe to study opera?"

"He was a playboy," Grandma Oh says. "I'm sure he was a smart man and had many interests, but, Haeja-ya, I really was too shy to talk with the man. I was a teenage girl, I knew nothing." Grandma has changed since our last visit to Seoul. Her emphysema consumes her, breathing and life are becom-ing too harsh for her. Now her hacking cough is less a signature of her conversation than a malady, and she hardly ever laughs her wonderful laugh. Her old face is drawn and sad, though every once in a while her old vigor returns and she races around only to fade a few minutes later, collapsing into a chair or a corner, like now, refusing to accept the modernity of this home. Her manner remains resolutely country, full of the old ways, but with the irritability and brittleness of old age. Lately she's taken to railing at Hae-Chul's wife, Ok-Hyun, and at the maids.

Most of the time she sits in her room upstairs, watching the dynastic soap operas. The ashtray at her side fills up with butts as the day goes by. Even the Turtle Ships with filters have proved too strong for her, so she now smokes Eunhausoo, "Milky Ways," the Korean version of low-tar and nicotine. She is depressed, lonely—old. Every time she speaks to Haeja, she tells her granddaughter that no one loves her.

"If I found a person who loved me," Grandma says, "I might die a happy woman."

"But I love you," pleads Haeja.

The main reason we are in Seoul in the middle of the winter is that Hae-Chul called Haeja in New York and said he did not think that Grandma had that much longer to live—perhaps we could visit Seoul in December? We came right away, of course.

"One person," chants Halmoni. A cigarette dangles from her mouth, and when it has burnt down almost to her lip she lights another immediately.

"Tambae," she says, offering me one. Haeja tells her that she loves her very much, but that she's becoming impossible, which is true. Like a child, Grandma returns to her chant.

"If I knew one person who loved me. . . ."

Occasionally she alternates it with a counter-refrain. *"Aigo,"* she says, "I am dying.

"This fucking country has turned to shit," she says. "I can't imagine what kind of lucky cunt that new president's mother had to produce a man like him. Other mothers see their sons prosper, but I have to spend my old age without a son because of that dirty fucking war. All I have are grandchildren who never visit me." She smoked as a rebellious teenager would in front of her parents, and the look on her face has the slightest hint of a smile. I will smoke and say horrible things, her face seems to say. I'll pout and brood, I'll make demands, I'll say things that no one else dares to say because I'm an old woman, and once I see one person who genuinely loves me in spite of all this, then I will die in peace. So there. If you tell me yes, I will tell you no.

Though I am appalled at how useless she has become, how purposeless she is in the household, I can't help but admire her status. Koreans nurture their elderly rather than shunting them away from the center of their daily lives. All she has to do is be herself, as irascible and unhappy as that self may be, and accept everyone's esteem for her. Americans would have sent her to a nursing home long ago. In a Korean household, she is not just tolerated, she is venerated as the great elder of the family.

Her wrinkled lips pucker around the Milky Way. She coughs and shakes her head warily.

"What a lucky vagina the new president's mother must have had to produce a son she can see every day, no matter what he does."

None of the ajima are surprised by her outbursts. They have heard her speak like this—and worse—many times, and not just since she became feeble and old. If she was famous for anything, it was for that big voice, and the uncensored good time she had in cursing everyone and everything, in being indelicate and irreverent.

Grandma moves to the table where she sits cross-legged, cigarette burning between tiny tar-stained fingers. She watches Haeja eat a breakfast soup of beef and scallions, cooked kim-chee and rice, hot sauce and bean paste. Birdlike and toothless, Grandma Oh subsists on rice and bean curd, mush, sprouts, and tea, but she complains when meat is not offered her, even though she can no longer chew it. As a gesture, a courtesy, she still wants it to be offered. Scowling, she pushes her bowl of rice away.

"I want meat. . . ."

"You have no teeth," says Haeja.

"Fuck it," Grandma says, "blame my luck. Everyone mis-treats me."

"I am taking you to temple," Haeja says. Halmoni's face brightens.

"Which one?"

"Your favorite," Haeja replies. "The one up on the moun-tain."

"When?"

"Right now." The old woman becomes uncertain; so much good news so quickly.

"Tomorrow," she says. "Or the day after tomorrow."

"Today is the best time," answers Haeja.

"My luck," Grandma groans.

"Come on," Haeja prods her. "We'll go right now."

"Give me some time to get ready," Grandma responds, and then smiles for the first time this winter.

In the living room Haeja sings the Queen of the Night aria. I drink in the sound as though it were rice and tea. Her shoul-ders, they say, to explain how a small woman can make such a big, rich, exquisite sound. She has Kyong-Sang vocal chords, full of Silla enchantments. She must have been born with it, because she smokes a pack of cigarettes or more a day and drinks alcohol, two habits that would ruin most singers. Then, too, she is Grandma Oh's granddaughter, and Halmoni is as small as you can get and has the biggest voice of anyone I have ever heard.

Grandma walks to the car jauntily, and the driver bows. She is happy, distracted; for once she does not have to curse any-one—her grandson's wife, her own life, the maids, the weather, the government. I sit up front with the driver, while Grandma sits in the backseat with Haeja. Grandma pats her hand and says, "Good girl." But it doesn't take long for her to get back on track.

"She does not take good care of my boy," Grandma says to Haeja, starting in on her granddaughter-in-law again.

"Nonsense," Haeja says. "Leave her alone, Grandma."

"Uppity bitch," Grandma spits, "thinks she's too good for me. My father was a magistrate. What is her father?"

"Grandma," Haeja says.

"No, no, no, no," Grandma says, "she is no wife for Hae-Chul."

No, no, no, no, Halmoni shakes her head.

Maybe because she is in such a good mood, Grandma Oh's rejections somehow sound positive. Her denials are a game, an old habit, something she doesn't really believe. Her no's are more sounds than meanings.

There is no wind, but it is cold—no birds in the trees, no leaves on the trees. No snow falling either, though snow from an earlier storm still blankets the ground. The streets are empty except for the soldiers everywhere, and the tanks. I feel like we are the only people outside.

On the outskirts of the city the streets become less ghostly; they are filled with women and children, students and workers bundled up against the cold. Steam wafts through the air; smoke billows out of chimneys.

"He will like this monk," Grandma says, nodding toward me. This monk is not vain, she says, not grave, no, he's wise. She talks on, so quickly and loudly that Haeja has no time to translate what I don't understand, and my shaky grasp of Korean excludes me. I think about the temples I have visited,

and the Catholic church down the block from the Lees' house
on Kao-hai-dong. The church always makes me think of Hem-
ingway's war-torn characters; lost, damned, beautiful, scraping
for a dram of faith in a godless world. The temporary faith I
search out in a church or temple has everything to do with
being an American in Seoul; it is peculiar to feel that there are
no atheists in foxholes, in trenches, on cold-war peninsulas.

The car banks to a stop on a hillside lane with Korean brick
walls lining both sides of the street. The street itself is cobbled
and slick, raked at a sharp angle. The incline is too steep and
icy for the car, so we will have to walk from here. I run around
to the other side of the car to help Grandma even before the
driver gets there. Haeja slips and grabs the door handle to keep
her balance.

"Be careful," I call to Grandma, then remember that she
understands no English. Haeja shouts to her; Grandma laughs,
coughs, sways alongside the car and latches onto my arm. She
wants to scoot up the hill, but Haeja calls for her to slow down
and wait.

"Take it easy," she yells to me.

"It's okay," I say in Korean.

"That's good," Halmoni laughs. As we climb the hill I can
sense Grandma's excitement growing. From this distance, the
tip of the temple's colorful roof is visible, as is the stone stepping path leading to the ornate reddish portal.

We're still within the city limits, but the feeling is very rural;
the buildings one and two stories, the streets old and unpaved,
or, like this one, cobbled. Even this far from the center of Seoul
the streets are congested, not with cars, but people. Babies play
in the street in front of their parents' shops, old women scurry
about with bundles on their heads. The air is pungent with fish
sauce, kim-chee, ginger, scallions, and garlic. A sooty charcoal

177

smell scents the air, of the spent briquets that heat the ondol floors. But, like everywhere else in Seoul, the streets are spotless—no garbage, no graffiti, no candy wrappers or cigarette butts.

Ajima barter with a fishmonger over a pile of silvery blue mackerel; at another stall, the old ladies banter with the greengrocer over winter melons or the huge apples and pears that are now in season. Peppers hang in bunches from the rafters of the little shop, and batches of garlic wreathes braided with hemp hang from tenpenny nails hammered into a post. An ancient woman, older even than Grandma, shepherds five small schoolchildren in front of her as she picks up a silvery gray, scaley, antediluvian fish, examines it, thumps it down, picks it up again, reexamines it, mutters, thumps, and bickers with the fishmonger over the price. Her brood—probably her son's or daughter's—are silent as they wait for her to finish her shopping. Their obedience seems absolute, as if it were the only way to behave. The fishmonger wraps the fish in an old newspaper.

Some young men sit at the tables of a café, watching us come up the path. Even though it's freezing outside, they wear summer clothing, seemingly indifferent to the cold. They are college age, but not students, not farmers either—they probably grew up on farms, then came to Seoul to join the masses of cheap laborers who are everywhere in Korea these days. Before the Kwangju Massacre this past spring they were essentially neutral; now they often seem belligerent, especially toward Americans—one of the changes I've noticed since our last visit, when to be American was still to feel blessed on the peninsula. After the massacre, many Koreans held the Americans accountable for General Chun's actions. Their rage was triggered by America's refusal to intervene in the uprising or in the response of the Korean military. As we thread our way past them, I find myself falling silent, hoping that I can pass for European or South American.

Still, these young men seem more surly than belligerent; they have the mannered punkness of a fifties street gang defending their turf. Nearly all of them wear what amounts to a uniform: navy blue workout pants with a white stripe down the leg and matching nylon warm-up jackets; white sneakers with the heel crushed down, turning them into slippers; T-shirts with university or sports team names on them. The whole ensemble could have been purchased in one of the city markets for under twelve dollars, and I have the feeling that it comprises their entire wardrobe. They look at us menacingly as we climb the hill, casting especially hostile smirks in my direction. One of the toughs nods hello as we go by, then another laughs and they all begin to speak animatedly.

"G.I.," one says, "No, no," says another. *"Yong-gook-saram,"* a third states: "An Englishman." They nod their heads in agreement.

The roadway is steep and slippery and I turn my attention to navigating Grandma Oh. The tension dissipates and we pass by without incident.

The multicolored walls of the temple come into view, the intricate scrolling and figures standing in sharp relief against the horizon. The roof is made of slate and slants upward, its tiles dazzling in the December light. Winter birds forage in the rafters and in the leafless branches of the trees in the courtyard.

Grandma bolts from us, sprinting up the stepping stones to the gate. Birds skitter in the rafters; mice race around the foundation. Grandma disappears briefly from sight, then reappears on the other side of the gate, bounding up the giant stone steps that lead into the temple. Haeja and I follow, but we are

179

still skittering across the frozen courtyard ground when Grandma reaches the temple.

I remove my shoes at the top of the steps before entering. My feet turn to ice the moment they touch the cold stone floor. Grandma laugh-coughs and mutters happily. She lights a jost stick and deposits money in a receptacle, then kneels and prays before the large though modest Buddha. Haeja joins her in silent prayer while I wonder what kind of prayer I can offer the Lord Buddha.

The Buddha has a big Korean head and slits for eyes; he sits cross-legged, meditating. O Great Buddha, I pray. Grandma Oh prays to you daily because she knows that she will die soon and she wants you to help her passage from this life into another life, or from this life into nothingness. O Buddha, comfort her. She's had a hard life. And my wife, Haeja, prays to you, and though I am a bad facereader and an even worse mindreader, I imagine she prays that Dr. Oh is comfortable, that he is warm.

Life is full of suffering, Grandma Oh might say, but that is because life is an impermanent state. We suffer because of desire, and enlightenment is the end of selfishness, ignorance, and desire. I had been surprised when I discovered that Halmoni's faith is a deep one, since I had never heard her speak of God; then I learned that there is no point in speaking of God because there is no beginning and no end. But when I compare the virtues of Buddhism with my own Christianity, I'm confused, because I can't reconcile her life with these precepts. Good Buddhists are compassionate, generous, benevolent, cooperative, and give service. And yet when I think about Haeja's story of her grandmother, I can see that these are still Halmoni's ideals; but old age, aches, and pains have blunted her pursuit of them. What I forget is that Korean Buddhism, like

Zen, is a practice, above all else, concerned with harmony and nature.

The harmony in Grandma Oh's life comes from how she resolved her own grief at the loss of a son with her obligations to raise his children. And, like her fellow Koreans, Halmoni's response to nature is through her earthiness, her rootedness. That she smokes, drinks, and curses may be antithetical to the puritanism inherent in many Western beliefs, but as long as Grandma Oh remains compassionate, generous, benevolent, cooperative, and gives service—or at least sees these virtues as something to strive for in her imperfect state—she is not going against the nature and harmony of her deepest beliefs. Finally, her belief system teaches that all humans are equal, for it was Buddha himself who said that kings are like poisonous snakes.

Grandma's belief is an old one, tracing its roots to the fourth century in Korea, by way of China. At that time animism was dominant among the common people, Taoism among the nobles. It would be hundreds of years before ordinary Koreans received the Buddha, and when the court adopted the new religion, they did so reluctantly, even indifferently, more to appease China politically than to seek spiritual enlightenment for themselves.

It was during the fourth century that King Pophung was said to have beheaded the monk Icha'don; instead of blood, white milk flowed from the severed head. Thunder rumbled in the cloudless sky, the earth trembled, and Buddha had come to Korea. Yet that first Buddhist miracle was taken to heart only by the nobles and the court, while the common people continued to practice their beliefs with fortune-tellers, animists, and shamans. But in those several hundred years that Buddhism traveled from the court to the common people, it absorbed many of the rituals and ceremonies of the folk religions, though it was not until the time of Won-Hyo—the seventh-century monk who discovered China by not going to China—that the religion spread among the commoners.

By the end of the Silla period and the beginning of Koryo, Buddhism was Korea's main religion, and it reached its zenith during the Koryo dynasty when King T'aejo declared that the court depended entirely on Buddha's benificence. This, too, is probably where the political corruptions of the religion started. Monks were exempted from military conscription and temples did not pay taxes. Over the years, temples became little fiefdoms on which power bases were built. Some temples even had their own standing armies to protect their holdings of land, servants, and art treasures, very much like the European world of certain popes. These excesses aided the Yi nobles in their attempt to eradicate Buddhism, replacing it with neo-Confucian values.

The differences between the Buddhists and the neo-Confucianists were profound. Buddhism proclaimed that man was sinful, saved only by the compassion and grace of Amitabha Buddha. Confucianism proclaimed man to be inherently good; the new leaders were civically inclined, placing ethics before spirituality. Buddhists were ascetic, placing the ultimate reality of Buddhahood before the illusions of the social world. To the new power elite of the Yi dynasty in Seoul, Buddhism robbed the country of young men to labor in the fields and staff the military, and corrupted women during the festivals. Stories of women carrying on sexual liaisons in monasteries with their lovers are legion, and in many of the stories the monks themselves are the lovers.

. . .

I come out of my musings, noticing that grandmother and grandchild have gone, and I race to put on my shoes. I can barely feel my toes. I follow Grandma Oh's great bluesy voice, which echoes through the monastery. She is making her way down the steep, railless granite slabs that lead to the monks' quarters with Haeja close behind. Each time Grandma takes a step with her left leg, it appears that she is going to keel over the side and into the courtyard, yet she holds her balance and descends, walking ducklike, cursing, shouting, fuming, laughing, hacking, and coughing. Haeja tries to keep up.

When she reaches the courtyard, Grandma walks off toward the refectory. Haeja follows, but I sit on a cold bench in the middle of the courtyard to wait for them and rest. Birds alight here and there among the rafters of the red, gold, and yellow pavilion. In the garden in front of me is an old bell, and behind it, a leafless maple tree, tiny and decked with snow. The sky is the color of a celadon vase. The high-rises of downtown poke up from the horizon, like a distant kingdom. A magpie alights on a pine; silently, it checks out the garden, the temple, then flies off. There are no voices here, no cars, no trucks, no buses, no school children, no punks, no toughs, no old ladies, no driver, no grandmother, no wife. Even the mice scamper around without sound, like shadows in the rafters. I can almost hear the building creak and settle.

For T'aego, the Koryo dynasty monk-philosopher-poet, *No* was the great Buddha word. No! What is it? he asked. Does a dog have Buddha nature? NO! No: it was the most sublime of words, and had connotations at once spiritual and political. A monk said *no* to the world, to that sensual realm which dis-

183

tracts man from his enlightenment, from his return to his original mind or nature, free of ideas, images, customs, manners, traditions, and responsibilities. Politically, *no* was a useful word for the invaders, for conquerors, for enemies. *No* to the Mongols, the Manchus, the Japanese, even the Chinese, to the decadent native emperors and nobles, to the strictures of the Confucian world; *no* to the shamans even, the folk healers, the animists; *no* to yin and *no* to yang. *No* to the Americans—as young people did after Kwangju. *No* echoed through the mountains in the various hermitages where T'aego lived in China and Korea; he said *no* to the winds at Three Corners Mountain. Saying *no* enabled T'aego to address the illusion of clouds and the reality of mountains, to commune with the rivers, to be consumed by the divine fire of wisdom, which a living Buddha embodied. *No* was not so much a negative as it was the emptiness of an utterance that allowed one to enter the plenitude of the Buddha. No, a dog did not utter *no*. This *no* is like a cat stalking a rat, like a chicken protecting its egg—like a grandmother expressing her joy at her grandchild for taking her to a distant temple in the dead of winter to pray.

Grandma Oh goes to fortune-tellers and shamans, but her "formal" religion is Buddhism. Yet, the temple she has taken us to is not her regular one. That one is back in Seoul, right up the hill from Samchung Park; her regular temple is part of the Pure Land sect, and this temple on the outskirts of the city is of the Son sect. Son is a precursor of Japanese Zen, and it evolved from the vagabond holy man Bodhidharma, a fifth-century monk who brought Zen from India into China. Like Zen, Son eschews sacred texts for meditation and reflection; the Chinese and Sanskrit words from which Son, Zen, and Zazen derive mean "meditation practice" and "quiet reflection." But Grandma Oh's sect, Pure Land, is probably the simplest of all the Buddhist practices. All a follower need do is say the Amitabha Buddha's name in order to attain buddhahood. Thus: Na-Moo-Ah-Mi-Ta-Bool. I remember this prayer well from the hours in the hospital before Fionna was born— the labor went on and on for hours, and with it Haeja's chant: NA-MOO-AH-MI-TA-BOOL.

But it is only the means that are different between Son and Pure Land Buddhism. Both aspire to enlightenment as an end; both derive from that fourth-century Chinese import known as Mayahana or Great Vehicle Buddhism.

Once again Grandma Oh shows great nunchi for my kibun; she reads my feelings sensitively and well. I happen to be attracted to, and fascinated, by Zen—and Son is an even richer and earthier form of that practice. What I like is the simplicity, and how important the sect considers insight and silence, two qualities attractive to many writers and artists I know. Son monks believe that the only way not to violate the truth is through intuition and quietude, and their so-called Three Jewels are the Buddha, the Teachings, and the Fellowship. And even though sacred texts are replaced by the value of insight and silence, a Son believer never contradicts his or her reason. Though the trappings may seem otherworldly, Buddhism is the middle ground, and among Korean monks a great deal of stock seems to be given to earthiness, even the funky and low-down, no doubt having to do with Son's spiritual founder, Bodhidharma.

I think I first heard of Bodhidharma while reading Jack Kerouac when I was a teenager, and for a time he replaced St. Francis of Assisi in my pantheon of spiritual heroes. He was reputed to have a red beard and blue eyes and he dressed like a hobo. Koreans have a special fondness for him and his cryptic remarks. Sitting in the garden, waiting for Haeja and her grandmother to come back, I can almost see the hobo-monk as he stands before the Emperor of China. The emperor asks him what is the greatest meaning of the holy dharmas, the Buddhist scriptures.

"What is the highest meaning of the great truths?" the emperor asks with great sincerity.

"Empty," Bodhidharma answers. "Devoid of holiness."

"Who is looking at me?" the emperor asks.

"I don't know," the Bodhidharma answers, not out of a hip arrogance, but from utter humility, one jazzman riffing off another.

It is almost impossible to explain my fascination with Bodhidharma, his oblique, resonating words and his enigmatic observations. Part of it, I know, is that he reminds me of the Wandering Jew, Norman Mailer's White Negro, and Kerouac's Dean Moriarity. His temperament and that of Korea's collective temperament seem to coincide so effortlessly at times, and his essence seems to appear and reappear in various monks throughout Korean history. I can almost see Bodhidharma in many of the great Koryo monk T'aego's remarks, like his observation that the scriptures are the shit left behind by barbarians.

Grandma Oh's voice penetrates my reverie. Arms waving, legs pumping, cigarette in hand, she wobbles through the courtyard, then out the gate and down the steep stone steps to the icy street. Pulling up the hem of her Yi dress so as not to trip on it, she moves with the vitality of a young woman despite her unsteady legs. She laughs and waves when she spots me, and the three of us work our way slowly and carefully down the steep hill, single file.

Gradually, Grandma becomes quiet, her energy spent. At the bottom of the hill, the driver rushes over to help her to the car. She collapses in a heap in the back seat. The heater is already going, and I slide out of my shoes and prop my feet on the ducts to warm them.

"Well?" I ask my wife.

"No monk," she answers.

"What happened?"

"He left town," she begins, but Grandma interrupts her, with a long roll of Korean, tapping my shoulder for emphasis. I nod appreciatively, although I do not understand a word she says. There is no running translation: Haeja translates when she is talked out.

"This young monk had his feet planted on a desk and talked on the telephone. Like he was a business executive out of the university, not a monk. . . ."

"Kurae, kurae," Grandma agrees, "That's right, that's right."

Then she sits up and pulls on Haeja's sleeve: "Tell Michael what an asshole that monk impostor was."

"I'm telling him," says Haeja.

"Tell him what a fool that boy was."

"I will," Haeja says.

"You tell him for me that young monk was a big impostor, nothing like the old monk—no wisdom, no experience, no sense of others."

"Grandma," sighs Haeja.

In the old days, a monk could be dismissed for engaging in sexual intercourse or theft, for claiming to be a holy man before truly attaining that state, or for killing another human being. Then, as now, there were no penalties for rudeness or disrespect to an elder, a violation of a social code that entails punitive measures in a Confucian world.

"Tell him," Grandma nudges her again. "Go ahead, tell him what happened."

"I'm trying to, Halmoni."

Grandma lights up a cigarette and stares out the window. "He is not the one. That one won't do."

"No," Haeja agrees.

"The old monk went off to Mi-Guk," Grandma says.

"He left the country," Haeja translates.

"For America," I answer.

"That's right," she smiles.

"He won't do," Grandma shouts.

"Please," Haeja says, shushing her.

"Beer-ker-ree," Grandma says.

"Berkeley," Haeja translates again. "He went off to Berkeley, California."

"Far out," I say, laughing.

"Grandma says you would have liked the old monk very much, but not this young one."

"The young one sounds like a bookie," I say, "with his feet on the desk and talking on the telephone like that." Haeja translates what I just said and Grandma looks up, smiles, laughs, pats my arm and says, "That's right. *Kurae.* He won't do." Then almost as an afterthought, she asks: "You like my temple?"

"Yes," I say.

"Good," she answers, and falls asleep.

SILENT
NIGHT

A log burns in the fireplace as Hae-Chul puts the last tinsel on the pine tree, the colored lights blinking, the Christmas ornaments shining bright. Haeja sings carols at the piano with Fionna and her two-year-old cousin, who is trying to conduct. Fionna, now four and a half years old, seems peeved. Grandma Oh sits on the couch, sipping a whiskey—not arguing with Hae-Chul's wife for once. The sliding glass doors look out on a winter garden where snow falls. The smell of turkey roasting in the kitchen wafts through the house. All of this is for the children, we adults agree, but it is only the adults who have childlike faces, seeing the snow in the garden, the log in the fire, the lights on the tree. Christmas is sublime, in the way it can be only for adults who are still wounded by the past.

I myself have never experienced a happier Christmas, thousands of miles away from my homeland, watching snow fall over Seoul, even while, at the base of the hill, soldiers man huge tanks.

Of my own childhood Christmases I remember my father drunk, my parents fighting, my umpteen brothers and sisters bickering. If the tree made it from Christmas Eve into morning—my oldest brother and father had a fondness for wrecking it during the night—I could expect, like clockwork, pairs of underwear and socks, and, in really flush times, a flannel shirt. Christmas evening, my drunken, red-headed Irish godmother would show up with her wimpy subway-token-clerk boyfriend. She would be good for laughs until she got too drunk and wanted to fight everyone, and she'd bring me a puppet or marionette or cap gun, which by the following morning—Saint Stephen's Day—was usually broken by one of the other children. No, I had no regrets spending Christmas in Seoul with the Oh and Han families.

Christmas Eve ends peacefully, and we go to bed, Haeja's singing still echoing in my head. Long after we are asleep, the ajima are busy working on the Christmas dinner that will be served at the Hans' next door. Where such items are found in Seoul, I do not know, but the menu includes cranberry sauce, sweet potatoes, and corn, along with the usual Korean festive dishes and condiments.

This stay, it seems, my focus has shifted away from the women's world of the house to the more Confucian realm of the men. By early afternoon, dinner is over and the cousins fill the living room, whose floor is carpeted with wrapping paper. Hae-Chul, Mr. Lee, and I excuse ourselves for a round of nine-hole golf. Outside, the day clear and dry, we load the bags and shoes into the trunk of Uncle Mo's car.

A Siberian cold has settled over Seoul. Snow blankets the

golf course, on the outskirts of the city, all nine holes within the oval of a horse-racing track, and I am given a half-dozen orange golf balls that can be identified in the white landscape of the fairway and rough. My game is poor until the eighth hole, when, stuck in a sandtrap, I chip out and the ball rolls into the cup. A birdie! By now, the foursome and the women caddies are bone-frozen, and we adjourn to the clubhouse to thaw out.

Inside the locker room businessmen on holiday talk shop with their associates. One or two generals sit on the benches in front of their lockers, attended to by lesser officers. Uncle Mo wants to know who is heavier, myself or Mr. Lee, and puts his money on Mr. Lee. We step on the scale, which reads in kilograms and renders me a few digits bigger than Mr. Lee.

"Too much beer," Uncle Mo jokes, tapping my newly acquired potbelly. Like a schoolboy in a gymnasium he ribs me about what he calls my "yellow" smell, and I explain that even in a Siberian winter, playing sports makes me sweat a lot.

"Powerful armpits," Uncle Mo says, holding his nose near me. "You could defeat a regiment of North Korean regulars with that weapon. Such a smell is banned by Geneva Convention."

I pick up a pair of Mo's socks and sniff them. "He talks. . . ."

"Poison gas," Hae-Chul says.

"Ah, poison gas," Uncle Mo nods. "That's very clever. Poison like my jokes."

"Exactly," Mr. Lee agrees.

"We must be spotless for the drinking house," says Uncle Mo. "You don't want to smell like a dog when you meet Seoul's lovely hostesses."

"True," Mr. Lee says.

"How true," Hae-Chul concurs.

I say that I bet they don't get this clean for their wives, trying to find where and how I'm supposed to banter with the men. I understand very little about the protocols of this world. Am I an honorary insider, or am I just being allowed a glimpse inside?

Uncle Mo suddenly looks quite serious. "Marriage is arranged," he explains. "A marriage is for children, family, family name, to continue our traditions. There is no romance in marriage, it's not like in the West. Marriage is a legal arrangement to make the best-quality children available by combining family characteristics in the best way possible. That is marriage."

"Romance," Hae-Chul snickers.

Mr. Lee finishes for him. "For most men, romance comes outside the home."

"This is so," agrees a businessman, toweling himself off.

A general adds: "All the responsibility of a life and a family and to a community and to the world falls on a man's shoulders. . . ." All shake their heads in agreement. The general continues: "What is the harm in a little fun?" He winks and they laugh. This is so, they nod, exactly so. What is the harm?

Nearby, another general gets into his spiffy uniform, attended by his assistants. He says: "The difference between a man and woman is this: men die in wars." Ah, yes, all nod affirmatively. Men die in wars. That being so, a man has a right to do anything he wants, knowing that he must fight the wars and make the greater sacrifices for his country. "It is that simple," the general says. Then he and the other general bow formally to everyone and walk stiffly out of the locker room.

I listen to these remarks as though I am hearing a Greek chorus, yet I am not sure if they are toying with me or telling me the truth. I am not entirely at ease in this male world, even though I grew up with six brothers whose only imperatives were knowing how to drink and how to fight. Yet, something like the harsh granite beauty of the mountains dwells in this masculine place. I wonder if men like Uncle Mo think that perhaps this is the way one speaks to Americans, as if all of us were John Wayne.

"We are all Kyong-Sang Province old boys," Uncle Mo laughs in the little cafeteria where we stop to drink beer and eat salted peanuts before going off to the drinking house. He has something of the beaten dog about his face and bearing, and I reflect that, even though he attended the military academy and knows people in high places, his illegitimacy robs him of the social credentials his two younger "relatives" carry with such ease.

Hae-Chul looks momentarily saddened. "If I had it to do over," he says, "I would go to the military schools like Uncle did, and to hell with Seoul National University, 'the Harvard of Korea.' If you want to become president, you must go to military school."

Mr. Lee's profound silence speaks his disapproval. "Enough foolish talk," he says at last, quietly, almost wistfully.

Uncle smiles, showing one gold-crowned tooth. "You will enjoy this little outing," he says.

Outside the clubhouse, his driver is waiting in a large black Korean sedan, and we drive back downtown to the area around Nam San, the mountain in the center of the city. It is colder now, and a light snow falls.

Uncle Mo is telling me about Nam San. "Poets loved to write about it in olden times. But then the Japanese built a Shinto temple on its peak, and one of the first acts of liberation was for Koreans to topple it."

Now the mountain is riddled with observation posts, military communications bunkers, TV and radio towers.

The black sedan winds down a narrow street lit with neon signs. I sit in the back with Hae-Chul and Mr. Lee. The seats of Uncle Mo's sedan have white and blue covers and pillows cross-stitched with the marital phoenix, *bong-hwang-sae.* The seat covers are like Uncle Mo himself, chintzy yet elegant, reflecting the tastes of a striver, a man who has yet to arrive. Looking out the window, I'm fascinated by the signs, the beautiful strangeness of the Korean script. As shamans talk of spirits in the earth, in mountains, in all things in nature, there is a kind of spirit in the neon, a quality of being alive, honky-tonk and Confucian, the flickering lights seeming to whisper over the night, Sin Sin Sin. . . .

The car stops in front of what looks like a fish house. At the entrance, we ring a doorbell and wait. A trim man in a tuxedo with a face like a Korean Clint Eastwood greets us and shows us in. A receiving line of employees makes formal bows as we move down a long, narrow hallway to a small room with couches against three of the walls, and a low Korean table in the middle. The walls are paneled in wood and hung with folk paintings. Near the door, there is a tiny dance floor, a microphone on a stand hooked up to a rhythm machine and a speaker, and an electric guitar leaning against the wall.

A woman with hennaed hair, wearing a leopard-print dress, appears. She says hello to us, then throws her arms around Uncle Mo, plastering his face with wet kisses. He peels her off, spins her around, and introduces his "relatives." He tells her that he is a lucky man since his relatives are also his good friends. Ah, she answers, as though he were very wise. Uncle Mo calls her his second wife, and she slaps his arm playfully. I realize that I have never heard him speak of his wife and children, although I am under the impression that they live in Hawaii or Los Angeles. Uncle Mo pinches one of her buttocks.

"Naughty man," she coos, and gives him another hug.

Hae-Chul and Mr. Lee shrug at each other.

"She understands me," Uncle Mo winks, grabbing one of her breasts and turning it like a doorknob. He lets out a feral laugh, a hoot and a howl. "Naughty boy," she says.

"Sit, sit," she scolds us and exits, her ass swaying.

A waiter brings in whiskey bottles, glasses, ice, nuts and seaweed, curds and fish. Salt seems to be the main ingredient in everything, to make us thirsty. But I like the Korean custom of never drinking without food, and I am quite hungry after the golf and the hot shower and bath. I also like that our bottles—whiskey, beer, or wine—are communal. Uncle Mo opens the first collective whiskey bottle, pouring large drinks for everyone. I explain that I'm not a good whiskey drinker and would prefer beer, but he insists I start with whiskey. His laugh is deep in his belly now. Hae-Chul and Mr. Lee look uncomfortable, but they drink off their whiskey with ease, and Uncle pours more. He wants to know why I have not drunk off mine, and I say that if I drink whiskey so quickly I will get very sick.

"But you are a great drinker," he says. "You are Irish, the Koreans of Europe."

"That's all right," Mr. Lee counters. "Let Michael drink whatever he wants."

"We will have a good time," Uncle Mo orders, downing his whiskey in one gulp and quickly pouring himself another.

"This is not a kisaeng house," he tells me. "It is not a drinking house. It is called a room-salon." Only old men go to kisaeng, he explains, and besides, there are hardly any women entertainers, in the traditional sense, left in Seoul. The old ones, he tells me, wrote poetry, and I say that I know that already. Then he tells me that his mother was a kisaeng.

"How do you say it," he says. "I am a bastard. A son of a bitch. . . . My mother was a gifted poet. But, today, people like yourself must write the poems. We are too busy with running the factories to worry about poetry."

The first time I met Hae-Chul we talked about morning calm, which he claimed was only good for people like myself— poets. "Businessmen like broken calm," he said. "That way we know that the factories are running."

"Let me tell you about my mother," Uncle Mo shouts, his voice rising out of control, but just then the door opens and four very attractive women, fashionably dressed, come into the room. Each takes a seat next to a man.

Uncle Mo lurches for the first girl, the homeliest of the group and the earthiest, her cheeks slightly pocked and flushed. He shows no more restraint than a farmer at a cattle auction: he grabs her breasts, pats her belly and buttocks, and runs his hands up and down her legs. The country girl laughs good-naturedly, as though such behavior is only an occupational distraction. Uncle asks the girl next to Hae-Chul how her grandmother is feeling. Quite well, thank you, she replies. Good, good, he says.

He pours the girl next to him a long shot, and she raises a toast to friends and relatives. All drink off the whiskey quickly, and none of the women flinches from the harsh taste. The country girl refills everyone's glasses as Uncle Mo comes over to me and aligns his profile with my own, then asks the woman sitting next to me if our faces do not resemble each other. She laughs at how large my nose is, even by Western standards. I think: Uncle Mo would be sensational at a used car salesmen's convention in Cleveland, and I realize suddenly that I am quite drunk.

Hae-Chul speaks, as if from the bottom of the bottle. Like the others, his face has turned a deep red and his eyes are watery and bloodshot, the characteristic Asian allergy to alcohol. But that doesn't stop him from drinking, though his English slurs, the words seeping out as if by no fault of their own.

"Uncle takes cabinet members here," Hae-Chul says.

Uncle Mo waves a finger in caution.

"Don't spread rumors," he says.

Now Mr. Lee, not quite so red-faced, leans toward me, and says in English, which is rare for him, "Malicious rumors, this is against our Yushin constitution. But Little Brother Oh is only joking."

"I am joking," Hae-Chul titters, with a broad, drunken smile.

"Not a joke," Uncle Mo frowns.

Hae-Chul downs his glass, not two or three fingers but more like a fist. He hangs his head, then speaks.

"I am going to send my son to military school," he laughs bitterly, "so he can become president."

"Now, now," Uncle says, "we are going to drink and hold our drink and act like brothers because we are brothers, and we are going to have a good time, and not complain about our stations in life, especially you, little brother, who is so rich and spoiled and well-educated and have never wanted for anything, you who went to the best schools and have your own business, a beautiful wife and lovely children. Before you are forty years old, you will be a millionaire several times over, so why grudge your uncle the small living he can make in this harsh life. . . ."

It is a lovely speech, full of twists and turns of locution, and Hae-Chul raises his glass to salute his "distant relative."

"To brothers!" the country girl shouts. Everyone applauds. Uncle Mo ritualistically drinks off his glass of whiskey, the country girl does the same, and around the room it goes. When my turn comes, I take it in one swallow, but I want to spit fire. The woman sitting next to me pours another round, and again we drink in turn. When it gets to Uncle, he opens the country girl's blouse and rubs whiskey on her nipples, licks it off, and she does the same to him. Am I drunk, or did the woman next to me also open her white silk blouse, baring her pear-shaped breasts, the nipples dark and warm, and did I rub whiskey on them and drink it off and did she do the same to me? My head spins, and I know that if I do not eat I will vomit. Though a good drinker, I'm poor at drinking games.

I lean drunkenly over the table, trying to steady the chopsticks in my hand, and spear a piece of fish. My partner slaps my hand lightly, takes the chopsticks out of my hand and with ceremony feeds me the salty fish. The food is delicious, and settles my inner ear's wavering, but when I come out of my reverie, I notice that everyone is looking at me, waiting. I shut one eye and a glass appears in my hand. It is at this point in the evening that I discover I have two left hands, two right hands, and everyone has two heads.

As though reading my mind, Uncle Mo tells a story.

"They say that Kim Il-Song, the Communist leader of North Korea, has a tumor on his neck so big that now it looks as if he has two heads."

I cannot stop laughing, though I know it is only because of the alcohol. I take only a sip this time and am instantly chided. Drink, drink, they say, and I drink. Now I'm sure that I am going to throw up and I go off to wash my face. Not only my head, but my stomach, too, burns now, from the whiskey and the spicy food. When I return, I hear my partner in the bathroom, vomiting. One by one, the men and women go to the bathroom to puke.

My partner comes out refreshed, hair combed, breath smelling of mint, lipstick and makeup neatly applied on her attractive face. I am not sure when it started or by whom, but I notice that fifties rock 'n' roll is playing, and the others are beginning to dance, singing along in Korean. My partner gestures for me to get up and dance with her.

On the dance floor, Uncle Mo announces that I am a writer.

"Let's hope he does not write badly about us," the woman with Hae-Chul says.

"Shee-in," Uncle Mo cries out. "Poet," he says.

"Ah." My partner bobs her head drunkenly in agreement.

"I am also a *saeng-son,"* I tell her in Korean, and she laughs uncontrollably. Is it my accent?

"What's the matter?" I ask Uncle Mo.

"You just told her that you are a fish," he says. "Naturally she finds it very funny that you are a fish. She thought you were an American."

"But I told her that I was also a teacher," I defend myself. "I didn't say that I was a fish."

"Ah," Mr. Lee laughs. *"Saeng-son*—that is fish. You said that you are *saeng-son.* You are a fish. You want to tell her that you are—"

"That you are *son-saeng,"* Hae-Chul interrupts, dancing with his partner. "That you are a teacher, too."

"Ah, ah," my partner nods. She looks relieved to discover that I am a teacher, not a fish.

As we dance I tell the woman that I'm translating Korean poetry—Hwang-Jini, Myong-Ok, Hongnang, all kisaeng poets—but she seems to understand nothing of my drunken patois. Finally Mr. Lee explains what it is I am trying to say. "Who is Hwang-Jini?" she asks.

Uncle Mo laughs from deep down around his groin. "Silly country girl," he says. The woman flushes. But one of her colleagues begins to sing what I realize is a poem by Hwang-Jini set to music:

> *Don't brag about your speed,*
> *O blue green stream running by the hills.*
> *After you reach landsend and the ocean,*
> *There is no turning back.*

"But that is Hwang-Jini," the woman with Hae-Chul shouts.

"Yes, yes, I know," the singer answers. "I know who wrote that song." She continues, as if in a trance:

> *I carouse all night*
> *In moonlit fields*
> *And return home to find,*
> *In my bed, four legs.*
>
> *Two of these legs,*
> *I have known as they slid*
> *Past my own two legs.*
> *Two of these legs,*
> *I have owned, but now*
> *They are taken.*

" 'Song of Cho-Yong,' " Uncle Mo shouts. Then to me: "You know that Silla dynasty poem?"

"Yes," I answer from my drunken haze. "That's one of the poems I've translated." I remembered that a spirit had inhabited Cho-Yong's beloved and that he had broken the spell by singing that poem. Uncle Mo is at my ear.

"Who is better than Kim Sowol?" he asks loudly. No one sits and no one dances; we reel about the tiny room drunkenly, clanging glasses, going off to the bathroom, bodies tilting and stumbling. Then my partner begins to sing.

> *When you go away*
> *'Cause you can't stand me*
> *I'll let you go gently*
> *Without a word.*
>
> *Azaleas of Yaksun, Yongbyon*
> *I'll gather an armful of them*
> *Pouring them on your path.*
>
> *Gently step on them, O*
> *Step lightly on the flowers*
> *Laid out for you, and go.*
>
> *When you go away*
> *'Cause you can't stand me*
> *I won't shed a tear*
> *Even though it kills me.*

Sowol's "Azaleas" was one of the first Korean poems I had ever translated, and it is one of the few I would recognize recited, although this is the first time I had heard it sung. The poem is sentimental, somewhere between William Blake and Frank Sinatra, and perfect for this Christmas evening.

The woman finishes and sips pensively at her whiskey, rubbing my back like a tired mother burping a child. She has turned inward, as though the room and the rest of us have vanished from her world. Soon her sad face and her sad recitation of the sentimental poem spreads to all of us, and a great sorrow veils the room, a hollowness that makes the evening timeless.

Now from the corner comes Hae-Chul's voice—singing "Arirang," Korea's unofficial national anthem, and the sorrow is everywhere, all of us weeping, for that is what Koreans do when they hear this song.

> *Arirang, Arirang, Arirang hill,*
> *We are going over Arirang hill.*
> *If you, my love, go along without me,*
> *Before you have gone a few miles,*
> *You will have sore feet.*

The microphone is passed around, and, to recapture our buoyancy, one of the women sings a medley of Christmas songs—"Silent Night," then "Oh Come All Ye Faithful," "Jingle Bells," "Jingle Bell Rock," and "Deck the Halls." I try to sing "Autumn Leaves," but I am one of the world's worst singers, even though I am married to one of the best, and someone else quickly takes over. Hae-Chul sings "Are You Lonesome Tonight?" giving it his Elvis best. When the microphone comes back my way, I try a Merle Haggard song, and everyone agrees this attempt is much better. I am encouraged enough to venture some Willie Nelson, but one of the women begins a reprise of "Arirang," and the sadness and sorrow wells up again in the drunken room. But it creates a kind of solidarity, and when the reddish-haired woman sings "I Want to Hold Your Hand," we all do, rocking back and forth.

Curfew brings an end to the evening, although one of the men suggests that we stay locked up in the room-salon all night. But the lights come up, and the Clint Eastwood manager enters the room to clear the table. Uncle Mo pays the lady in the leopardskin dress and tips each of the women. We find our coats and are escorted to the door, where each of us is given a bouquet of lollipops and flowers, and sent out into the night. Drunkenly, we reel along the slippery alleyway, looking for Uncle Mo's car. When we find it, Uncle Mo takes the driver by the lapels.

"A good man," he says, shaking him. "This is a good honest man. My friend."

The nighttime street is empty. Snow falls quietly and there is no wind, but the temperature must be around zero. We pile into the car, Uncle Mo sitting in the front.

"I am a man," he says.

"That's right," Mr. Lee answers him.

"A man," Mo repeats.

"He is a man," Hae-Chul repeats, too.

"I am," he says.

"He is," I agree, and this makes everyone laugh.

"But if I were a woman," Mo says, "if I had breasts, if I had a vagina, which I don't, I don't have a vagina, but if I bled once a month until late into my middle age, if I bore children, if, like Lady Hwang, I watched a son die, if I raised my daughters the way a mother does, if I had to stand behind a screen so that men could rule in this Confucian world, if my sex drive did not peak at eighteen like us men, if it burgeoned until I was forty-five or fifty or fifty-five or sixty, if it did not diminish in my prime—the horniest women in the world are forty-two-year-old mothers who have never been unfaithful in their lives—if I grew my hair long, wore lacy underwear and underclothes, if my dresses were colorful and long, if I were a poor woman who worked in a kitchen, beating clean, wet laundry with a stick, if I were a rich lady like Lady Hwang, this awful goddamn awful Lady Hwang, if I were fucking Hwang-Jini herself, if I was Hwang-Jini, if I were educated and creative, a woman outside the society of other women like my own mother was, my dear goddamn mother, my sweet goddamn mother, my poor mistreated Kyong-Sang mother, if I were like my mother who only was there to comfort men with her professional hands, her professional lips, her professional smile, her warm tender eyes, a woman who had the company of men but was not a man herself, if I were a woman who did not go off to war to die but stayed home and felt the absence of the men who died in war like Grandma Oh, like Grandma Oh, like the good and wonderful Grandma Oh, ah that woman is a saint, a martyr, a real Korean woman, that is Lady Oh, if I were a woman who knew that in other centuries I could be sold at market like a bolt of cloth or like a rubber shoe, like a cache of rice or like a side of beef, if I covered my body, if I bowed my head never lifting my eyes, if I walked with tiny steps in shoes the size of cucumber seeds, if I cursed the gods for who I am, a woman, if I cried over spring flowers, if I spit on passing jeeps, if I were one of many kisaeng, if I were a bar girl in a drinking house. . . ." But then Uncle Mo throws his head forward into his hands, he weeps, and the three drunks in the back do not notice, because the strange and funny music of alcohol rings in our ears. Uncle Mo cries as Hae-Chul sings another Elvis Presley song. Then Mr. Lee hums a popular Korean song that I have been hearing every day on the radio. I throw my head back and dream a ridiculous dream about kisaeng, about Hwang-Jini.

AN ORDINARY DAY IN SEOUL

When I wake up, the room is suffused with the bluish half-light of morning. Haeja sleeps next to me with Fionna next to her. I look around the room. I am in the bedroom of the Lees' house, down the road from their old traditional one. This is one of the few rooms that I've immediately known where I am on awaking, the furnishings so different from anything I have seen before or since.

The ondol floor is made of yellowed rice paper and oil; the sleeping mats, which are laid out on the floor at night, are a florid purple, the starched quilts, pink and pale green and pastel blue, the pillow white and starchy and boxy hard. There is a long, low table by the window, a Western-style dresser in a corner, and a pair of high black and white mother-of-pearl Korean chests on the far wall. Near the door are two wall-length, glass-doored bookcases filled with encyclopedias in

Korean and English, guides to French and engineering, dictionaries and college yearbooks, family albums and college texts, miscellaneous English books of unknown provenance, mysteries, best sellers, self-help, thrillers, sci-fi, and one Louis L'Amour cowboy novel that I probably left behind a few years ago. The walls and ceiling are covered with a floral wallpaper, rose and tan on a cream background.

After the three of us get up, the old ajima comes in to stack the mats and quilts and pillows in a corner. Squatting, she cleans the floor with a damp cloth, takes out the garbage, collects our soiled clothes and goes down stairs to do the laundry. She was hired years ago as a companion for Grandma Oh, and when Halmoni died last year she stayed on as a helper for Hae-Soon and her children. She is stooped with age but has a cheerful, open smile. The youngest of her six children works downtown as a secretary for the Hans' company.

In the early morning, the pearly gray *mae-mi* whir and buzz, their insistent cicadan singing a constant chorus during these late summer days. The insects are quiet in the night, and it is only in the first light of morning that one becomes aware of them starting up, almost like an orchestra tuning up before a performance. Soon their song is a white noise in the background that is impossible to notice. Only rain hushes them; as soon as it stops, the *mae-mi* vocalize with even greater intensity. At the moment, it is raining and the air seems to ring with their silence.

Beyond the garden wall, below in the street, some old men talk and chant as they head to the park for their morning exercise. Their throaty voices fade as they move on, then the rain picks up, splattering the trees, the roof, and the concrete street below, until it reaches a crescendo and subsides. A dominion of birds takes hold of the air, mostly sparrows and finches in the pines in the front yard; in the softness of the birdsong, the rain gently returns. Across the street and up the hill someone is playing a scratchy old jazz recording, and a saxophone solo adds a cadenza to this ceremony of the first light of morning. Then the blue notes of the sax are drowned out by a chorus of monks chanting and playing their clappers. The wheels of a car slide over the slick pavement, the transmission grinding as the car approaches the incline of the hill, moving northward. The birds return to their song, the rain begins again, then more old men and now school children, mothers, ajima, soldiers and other young men, and I know that the day has truly arrived.

I sit in the living room with Haeja and Hae-soon, watching the rain as they gossip about this and that. Fionna is upstairs playing with her cousins, and my nephew brings in a portable chess set. Sitting across from me, he lingers forever over his moves, then usually catches me off guard with some fancy trap. He's twelve years old and should be man enough to accept defeat but so far he has done nothing but win game after game.

The monsoon season has persisted longer than usual this year, and so even this late in the summer it is sticky and wet outside, and the air-conditioning is turned on in the living room. Unfortunately, I am usually here during the summer months, which are hot and humid and rainy, day after day. Spring and fall are the best seasons, and winter, though often brutally cold, is invigorating with its windless Siberian chills. But New York City is hotter and stickier in summer than Seoul and the trade-off is worth it—here at least I am treated as an honored guest. Moreover, Seoul is where I gather myself, where I put myself back together. Here I don't have to worry about work, or laundry, or picking up Fionna from school. Left to my own thoughts as the rest of the family catches up on one another's lives, I become expansive, philosophical.

The two older sisters' voices become animated and musical as they talk. Back in each other's sphere, they lose their Seoul accents and revert to the slower, more cadenced rhythms of the south. As the drawl becomes more pronounced, they sound more and more like southern belles.

Upstairs, the cousins speak broken English with their young relative from New York. Fionna was an infant when she first came to Seoul, and the first visit she remembers is in fact her second; she was nearly five and had to defer to an outrageous male cousin who was in the throes of the terrible twos. Now she is almost a teenager, tall and stately like her oldest cousin. Her cousins are practicing their English, the oldest one in preparation for a big exam, but Fionna is not helping much, since she speaks too colloquially, using idioms the girls have not yet acquired.

"You see," she tells her cousins about a classmate, "she was wearing this dizzy hat, you know, and her hair was gooped up with mousse, and she had on a pair of pink Converse hightops, you know, trying too hard and kinda tacky with this beach-buggy yellow halter and this really *bad* polka dot skirt, but she was still the class nerd no matter how hard she tried. Really *droll,* if you know what I mean."

My nephew and his father have little interest in speaking English, but even they attempt a few expressions.

"I like your green suitcase," Chul-Hee says, smiling, but my suitcase is blue, and since it's so beat up and ugly, I have to presume that his remark is rote vocabulary he learned in school. For my part, I'm trying to reacquaint myself with Korean.

During a brief hiatus from the rain, I go out in the garden

to see what Seoul is like when the monsoon dies down. Listening to the birdsong, I discern jackdaws and magpies, and a few migratory birds already heading south to warmer climates. When the cold comes here, it comes quickly, and the birds know to fly before the Siberian elements descend. Less than an hour's drive north, at the DMZ, some of the most unexpected and rarest birds in the world are found, even eagles, and outside of Seoul, pairs of cranes are a common sight in the paddies. But on this stay I'll be city-bound except for a brief visit to the country to attend a memorial service for Grandma Oh. We have come for this service and for two other important ceremonies—a niece's first birthday and Mrs. Han's sixtieth.

I have noticed that under martial law, perhaps because the only Americans I run into here these days are soldiers, the English I speak in Korea has become more peppered than ever with military jargon. Lifers, commissaries, REMFs, klicks, being "stationed" here, yes, sir, no, sir, bird colonels and buck privates, louies, katusas—these tumble out of my mouth in conversations on the street, in the lobbies of the hotels and in the markets near the American sector, to the south. Yet, inside the house the atmosphere is anything but military, it is so familial, peaceful, civilized, domestic that one might not think of the restrictions—except that the tear gas drifts down from Songgyun'gwan University nearly every day, seeping under the doors and through cracks in the windows, making everyone's eyes red and teary.

The sisters go downtown to do errands; the cousins are upstairs playing, Mr. Lee is off on business, and I am left to my own devices. I decide to take a cab to Itae-Won to shop. I ask the driver to let me off near Victory Market, then work my way down one of the alleys, squeezing through the crowd of Korean merchants in stalls, at carts, in storefronts, past the Americans from the Eighth Army base, who like myself, are looking for bargains. But today I am looking for a new pair of running shoes and a full-length leather coat. I usually come to Itae-Won to look and listen, not necessarily to buy, but sneakers and men's wear tend to be good values here.

I manage to squeeze past the clot of people at the mouth of an alleyway and work my way down a set of stairs into an underground arcade of little shops and booths, men's suits, sporting goods, and lots of leather merchants. In one shop a large, middle-aged black man is buying exactly the kind of coat I'm looking for.

"Been coming here for over twenty years," the soldier says, noticing me. "Only place around that has our size."

He nudges me in the belly and nods knowingly.

"Going back to the world for a visit," he says.

"Where's home?" I ask, detecting a northeastern inflection in his voice.

"New York," he says. "Harlem."

I tell him that I live up around Columbia University and we talk about the neighborhood until the tailor comes back. Luckily for me, the soldier bargains a good price, and since I am in his presence when the deal is made, I know I'll get the same.

After making my purchase, I go back out to the main street and walk a few blocks to Victory Market, which is the hangout for American-raised Korean kids. I've begun to notice them in numbers this visit. They are usually of high school or college age, and have grown up partly in Korea but mostly in the United States. They speak some Korean, but their accents are distinguished by the American regions from which they hail. They are affluent, well-educated, privileged. They are less expatriates in the United States than they are visitors here. They are on vacation in their motherland, so they take language courses at the university, travel to the countryside to visit temples and ruins, and immerse themselves in Korean culture, but there is nothing of Confucian right-relationships about them. Rather, they project all the authentic rebelliousness of American teenagers. They buy dope from American soldiers in the Eighth Army, and their hairdos make a statement. Despite their features, their rhythms are not of this Asian city. I imagine that Korean parents driving by probably point them out to their children as examples of what will happen to them if they're not good.

On the way home, I stop at the Hyatt for a beer, a bite to eat, and most of all the fabulous view of the city to the south, toward the Han River. I come to see this every time I'm in Seoul—somehow it is central to experiencing this city correctly, and it is this view that stays most in my mind when I am away. The newer hotels are nice enough, but this one is perched on the side of Nam San, over the ever-increasing sprawl of shacks, shanties, and villas; beyond the river one can see clusters of high-rise apartment buildings.

My eyes and nose are burning again, and I think I may be catching the flu, but when I get home I discover that everyone else's eyes are burning and tearing too. More tear gas, and worse than usual with today's down-draft. The gas brings back memories of the sixties and antiwar demonstrations. Last week a professor told me over drinks that there were days when the tear gas made it impossible for her to teach; one day, she said, she'd had to cancel a lecture because she realized on approaching the podium that she simply had no voice.

I have picked up more Korean for this trip, though I still speak the language like a village idiot; I have vocabulary, it seems, but no grammar, or if I speak grammatically, I have no feel for the social order built into the language, no sense of the formality and decorum of this Confucian tongue, the orders, the right linguistic relationships.

This evening I am to go with Hae-Chul and his friend Sleepy Pai to a raw-fish house in Yong San in the center of the city. While I wait for him to pick me up, I write letters and listen to my language tapes, repeating basic phrases. The house is quiet. The children are playing badminton in the garden, the sisters are talking in the dining room, and the ajima are making dinner in the kitchen.

The restaurant is a Korean place not frequented by tourists, and it turns out that I'm the only American. It is a small place, tucked away down a network of alleys. Its exterior is modest, timeless, and unremarkable. There are a few small wooden tables and chairs along the back wall, where the owner works with his assistants. Hae-Chul is a bit of a big shot here, and everything stops when he walks in. We sit, and I submit to being fussed over by the owner, the waitress, and the assistants. We begin with an array of eel, squid, tuna, and a small fish that looks like a sardine and tastes like herring, washing down the sashimi with Korean wine—*majuang*—which is quite good.

The sea is never far from any sensation or experience in Seoul. An ordinary walk through the market brings smells of dried octopus and squid, cod and bass, the stalls filled with fish roe, long strands of dark green and salt white seaweed, fish sauces, baby clams, mussels, and oysters from Cheju Island when they're in season. Sometimes the briny smells of Seoul's back alleys and street vendors, its basements and shops seem almost as strong a link to the place as my marriage to Haeja. No matter how many high-rises and office buildings and subway stations and modernized cars clog its rhythm, Seoul is always salty and down-to-earth. Heaven's above, sure, but Earth is right here, and Man, too, moving by obstinacy and will against the gravity of this place.

The next course consists of abalone chowder, squid salad, roots, *nurungi* (bottom-of-the-pot sugared rice), sea bass, white fish, tuna underbelly, and fish roe. The majuang flows, and the supply of food seems endless. The chef-owner dreams up new combinations and concoctions every couple of seconds, and each manages either to complement what preceded it or to whet the appetite for what is to follow. There is a sense of ritual to the meal, despite the ordinariness of the place.

"Jae il," I say, meaning, Number One, a high compliment, and my words are not idle.

The chef is pleased that his good customer Hae-Chul has brought a foreign guest with such an appetite for what he does so well. He carves a piece of raw squid so that it looks like a miniature squid and places it in front of me. Hae-Chul uncorks another bottle of majuang. The waitress hovers in the background and sees to it that our glasses and plates are always filled.

Several hours pass this way before we decide we can eat no more. Hae-Chul pays—by now I've learned that my protests are only a formality—and the owner sees us to our car, where the driver has been waiting. The chef opens the doors for us and bows deeply. We promise to return.

We drive southward, heading over the Han River and into New Seoul, but the three of us have had so much to eat and drink already to even think of stopping at a drinking house. When we get back to the Lees' house, we take refuge in the air-conditioned living room, with a scotch for Hae-Chul and a cold beer for me.

For the first time this visit I hear a sonic boom. By now I

know that it's a reconnaissance rocket, but I've assumed it was unmanned. This evening Hae-Chul enlightens me: It flies out of Okinawa, he says, at Mach three, possibly an A-1, certainly manned. Technically its area of operation is South Korea, but it flies from the DMZ up to the Yalu at the Chinese border and back in twenty minutes, and at such an altitude that neither the North Koreans nor the Russians nor the Chinese are able to shoot it out of the sky. Once the North Koreans recorded a hit, only to discover that the rocket had scrambled their radar, and the anti-rocket fire had hit a ghost target.

This bit of military pontification pleases Hae-Chul no end, and he pours himself another fist-high shot of whiskey before he continues. But then he changes gears and launches into his theory of how the Koreans are going to do, first, in the Asian Games, and then in the Olympics—behind the Chinese but ahead of the Japanese. I am able to follow his Korean for a while, but as the night progresses, his words come faster and faster, colliding with each other. I excuse myself to go upstairs and pack, and to get some sleep. Tomorrow we are off to the Hans' for Byung-Su's daughter's first birthday. We will return a few days later for Mrs. Han's sixtieth birthday, and will end our visit with a drive into the countryside to pay our respects at Grandma Oh's gravesite.

Lying on my sleeping mat upstairs, I realize how much Korea has changed each time I've visited. The first time, in 1978, Kimpo seemed like a backwater airport, with one hangar and a windsock. Now it is a huge, modern hub. But this trip the changes seem less tangible. Certainly the student demonstrations have taken on a new coloring. Downtown, for the first time, there is heavy security around the American embassy and compound. I turn off the light. In the pitch black, the voices downstairs are only a distant murmur, reminding me, as I drift off, of the whirring and buzzing of the mae-mi.

Outside the window, I hear the faintest rustle of the wind, then the spat-spat of raindrops on the big paulownia leaves, and everything goes silent under the rain.

THREE CEREMONIES

"I am tired of this silly custom of not smoking in front of elders," Cousin Yoo says. "I am getting old myself."

Silence drifts over the room as he lights a cigarette.

"You can drink with an elder, and even make a fool of yourself. Why not smoke in front of them too?" Still, no one says anything.

"My children," he says, "they will be allowed to smoke in front of me."

"But they should never smoke," a niece says. "It is bad for the health."

"True, true," he concedes, to everyone's relief.

Cousin Yoo is one of Haeja's relatives on her mother's side. His mother is the sister who went into business with Mrs. Han after the war, raising five children by herself after her husband was kidnapped by the North at the outset of the Korean War.

Though considered the smartest in a family whose father was a renowned scholar and intellectual, Cousin Yoo had to end his education abruptly, because he was the oldest son, and so had to help his mother to support his brothers and sisters. Like many other self-made men, he is gruff and macho.

Dark-faced and stocky, Cousin Yoo appears impatient with many of the old ways, a person no longer comfortable with the easy rhythms of the old customs and ceremonies. As a businessman (he manufactures sneakers for different American and European companies), he is familiar with men from many different places in the world, and his sense of practicality makes him question what everyone else takes for granted.

"Why have a one-year-old ceremony?" he asks. "Why have a sixtieth birthday party? Why?"

"It is the custom," says Hae-Chul.

"That answer is not good enough for me, Cousin Hae-Chul."

"Why do we eat and drink? Why do we fuck? Why do we fart? Why do women wear dresses and men wear suits and ties? Why do we breathe?"

"That is my point," Cousin Yoo says. "Why?"

"That is life," Hae-Chul answers. "It is what makes us Korean and not French."

I have always been under the impression that the one-hundred-days and the one-year celebrations had to do with a time when Korea had a high infant mortality. Because children were vulnerable to fatal diseases, mothers kept them cloistered for the first hundred days of life, and when the child reached one year old, the celebration was a way to give thanks for his or her survival. But I realize that Cousin Yoo knows all this. He is asking why all the formality, not why these times are celebratory.

"You see," Cousin Yoo says somewhat kiddingly to me,

"asking *why* is not a hostile question. It is a good journalist's question."

Besides being a businessman who travels the world, Cousin Yoo has serious hobbies that almost amount to secondary professions. He is a scratch player in golf and his drinking buddies are all journalists. Many times he has invited me for drinks with his friends; an equal number of times he has told me that I must write a book about the family.

"But what about the sixtieth birthday?" he asks.

"That has to do with the Chinese calendar," Hae-Chul says. "Every twelve years is a new cycle in the zodiacal calendar. Multiplied by six, it was considered a full life."

"Why?" Cousin Yoo asks.

"Why sixty was a full life?"

"Yes."

"I don't know," Hae-Chul admits. But then Byung-Soon sits down next to her sister, Byung-Ju. She explains that few people lived to be sixty in the old days. When you reached that age, it was thought that your life cycle was complete. "Then you were permitted to start a new cycle," she says. "In the old days, the Taoists made longevity a virtue because so few people attained old age. If you did, you must have done something well. The Will of Heaven must have looked well on you for your virtue."

Cousin Yoo smiles, a vindicated man. His gruffness evaporates, replaced by the gentleman-scholar's peace. Suddenly I see why Haeja considers him the kindest, most charming one of all her male relatives. Up to now, he has always struck me as a dark, brooding, moody sort of guy, who learned to play golf doing business in Vietnam during the American war there and who learned to be the head of a household long before he finished puberty.

He and I go into a back room off the kitchen where the older male relatives are gathered, drinking soda and whiskey and beer, smoking cigarettes. The room is smoky, the speech male—gravelly and from the belly. But we are not here for another meeting of the men's club. Rather, the various relatives have gathered at the Hans' for Byung-Su's daughter Kyung-Mee's *dol,* her first birthday celebration. In Korea one is considered to be one year old at birth, and thereafter everyone takes New Year's Day as their birthday. But the only birthdays that are celebrated, as Cousin Yoo pointed out earlier, are the first, *dol,* and the sixtieth, the *hwan-gap.*

Less than wanting to know the reason *why* these celebrations exist, I want to see *how* they are done. Of course, Fionna had had a one-hundred-day and a first-year celebration, Korean-style, wearing a traditional Korean outfit on both occasions, but that was back in New York, with no relatives present but her mother and father. Asking *why,* I realize, is like asking why Americans celebrate Sweet Sixteen or why they forget how old they are after twenty-nine; or why they make such a big deal about all those birthdays between one and sixty.

At a low table, the families' drivers play chess. At another, Cousin Yoo gets into a game of Paduk, or Go, with Byung-Jeen, who is a professional-level player. Byung-Jeen is a great gamesman. He is still not married, and lives a bachelor's life. Although involved in the family businesses, his love-obsession is Go.

The black and white stones are slapped down quickly and ceremonially—a sound that I have come to associate with being in Seoul. Most of the others are watching a Korean wrestling match on the television. There has been a renewed interest in traditional Korean sports in anticipation of the summer Olympics.

"Our goal," Cousin Yoo explains, "is to place ahead of Japan." He does not know that for the past week Hae-Chul has been saying the same thing.

Kyung-Mee is off being dressed in traditional costume for the ceremony, but over the television and the games, I cannot hear the women or the children in the other rooms. The air is thick with smoke, garlic and fermented cabbage. Some of us sit in chairs, but most sit on the ondol floor, one leg tucked under a buttock, the other leg propped up, the knee a small mountain peak, boddhisattva-style.

The talk has been about the Olympics, and when it is directed to me, it is about how the Korean boxers were robbed of medals by the officials. "I had nothing to do with those decisions," I remind the men. "In fact, during the last Olympics in Los Angeles, I was here in Seoul."

"All of us were vacationing in the Sorak Mountains," Mr. Lee corrects me.

"That's right. I watched the Olympics on a television in the lobby of the Hotel Sorak." When the subject drifts away from the raw deal the Korean boxers received in Los Angeles, invariably it goes back to archery, wrestling, and Ping-Pong, sports that Korea is expected to do well in. But there is also conversation about the export of Hyundai cars to America, and even a subject I never heard spoken of except in small, private conversations—democracy. Korea has changed so much in the last decade that what was once taboo in conversation, even in the household, is now discussed as freely as what is for dinner that night.

"President Chun's family must have invested heavily in tear gas," Hae-Chul says.

"They've got their money in stop lights," says Cousin Yoo. "That's why Seoul has so many now." When Park was in power, people kept their thoughts, political and otherwise, to themselves; but with Chun, it seems, everyone feels free to express their opinions. The negative reaction to him is especially strong among young people, but it is shared by much of the middle class, and even by the older generation. It would be difficult to find a people more alienated from their government than South Koreans were under him.

Now President Chun is gone, too. Last summer, the student rioters were joined by workers and a new protest group—the middle class. Elections were held, and Chun's colleague, former general Ro (pronounced No) Tae-Woo was elected in Korea's first democratic elections by thirty-eight percent of the votes. He accomplished this thanks to the personal rivalries of the two opposition candidates, Kim Dae-Jung and Kim Young-Sam. Though it was said the elections were not rigged, nearly everyone I meet in Seoul nowadays tells me that they voted for Kim Young-Sam. But President Ro, even if a former general like the two previous presidents, will no longer be able to stage a one-man show in South Korea: democracy really has caught on, following in the footsteps of the economic growth and the power of the media. Yet even if everyone speaks openly about politics now, the topic is second to the Olympics.

The black and white Go stones are slapped down hard and fast by Cousin Yoo and Byung-Jeen. The current game is intense, the stones echoing through the smoky back room, the players' faces becoming singular in their focus. Byung-Jeen often reminds me of a character in a novel; he is eccentric, stubborn, and differs slightly from everyone else's philosophies and life-styles.

"Koreans are industrious and hardworking people," Byung-Jeen says. "All of them," he laughs, "but me."

"You are the family's great Go player," the cousin tells him.

"Yes," he agrees, "Go is my mistress."

One of the maids knocks on the door. She does not dare enter this male warren, but shouts from behind the closed door: "Come to the living room, please." The celebration is about to begin. One by one the men wander out, fixing their ties, putting on their suit jackets, stuffing out their cigarettes, until only Byung-Jeen and Cousin Yoo are left, slapping down the black and white stones. Slap, counter-slap, slap, counter-slap. . . .

Kyung-Mee stands in front of a low table in the living room, looking terrified at all the attention lavished on her by the adults, many of them people she has never seen before in her life. She is a pretty little girl with a bright, inquisitive face. Her rainbow-sleeved, silk hanbok makes her look like an Yi princess. I marvel at the fact that this ceremony is very much the same as it was for her own parents, and in turn for Mrs. and Mrs. Han when they were infants, and for their parents, on back through some earliest moment in Korean time, when the idea for the ceremony first took hold. Byung-Su's daughter has survived the dangers of the first one-hundred days effortlessly, and then raced through the next nine months with equal dexterity. Of course, it does not hurt to have a doting mother and grandparents, adoring aunts and uncles, a loving bunch of cousins, and a father who is a doctor.

In front of her are a noodle, a thread, money, books and pencils. Which object she chooses will symbolically determine her fortune in life. If she goes for the noodle, she will always have enough food. Thread will guarantee a long life; money, obviously, signifies wealth. And if she chooses the books and pencils, she will become a scholar. That last choice suggests to me that the ceremony has its origins, not so much in ancient

Korean history, but in the Yi dynasty, where the scholarly way was the highest aspiration of a life. Kyung-Mee looks scared to death now.

Her father and mother have come up from the country this morning. After finishing medical school, Byung-Su has had to give several years to the military, and they are stationed at an obscure base two hours south of Seoul. The girl's relatives have gathered from all corners of the Earth for this occasion—one from New York, another from Cambridge, Massachusetts, one from the Philippines, another from the other side of the mountain here in Chongro-ku. There are streams of cousins, aunts, and uncles, young and old, too many to count.

The little girl remains still, unsure and scared. Finally, when it seems that she is about to cry, Mrs. Han kneels down next to her, takes the child's hand, and guides her tiny fingers to each object in turn.

"Let her decide when she grows up," Mrs. Han says. "Then she'll know which of these is most important." Everyone applauds and the little girl breaks into tears and rushes into her mother's arms. Byung-Ju, who is back visiting from graduate school in America, whispers: "Mother is right. This way her granddaughter will be rich, have a long life, never go hungry, and become a great scholar." Though the two youngest Han sisters rarely agree on anything, Byung-Soon acknowledges her youngest sister's observation.

Standing around chatting with the family, I realize that I've been here five or six times in the last ten years. When I first arrived, Byung-Ju and Byung-Soon were just out of high school; now one of them is married and a mother, and the other is in graduate school at Harvard. Byung-Chul, the baby uncle, is now the size of a point guard on a professional basketball team; his school days over, he thinks of marriage and a career in broadcasting. The size of the Han family has doubled with children, so that now there are more of the younger than the older generation, and to this mass of children I am now part of that older one, too. Since I was last here two years ago for another family excursion to the Sorak Mountains, five more babies have been born. Family remains the one constant in everyone's lives.

Though I find these gatherings predictable, a bit too formal, and even a little boring, I have to admire how the family works so hard to retain some of the older rituals and ceremonies. But Mrs. Han's intervention in the dol is an indication of how the role of these ceremonies has changed. They are performed out of habit, and provide an opportunity for the family to gather together. But they are also a way to honor some old traditions for their own sake, to provide an antidote for a too-modern world. In that sense, these rituals are neither quaint nor super-stitious, but contemporary and celebratory. It is no longer a question of celebrating the first year of a child who survived in a world of high infant mortality, for Korea has made incred-ible progress in this regard, but rather passing on to this child a custom that generations on generations of Hans have prac-ticed with their children. Yet, as important as the ceremony seemed when it was taking place, now that it's over, it seems nearly forgotten immediately.

The little girl has changed into more comfortable clothing and now plays with her cousins. The women sit on the couches, gossiping among themselves, while the men have wandered back to the gaming room to continue with Go, chess, and watching sports on television.

Two days later is Mrs. Han's hwan-gap, her sixtieth birth-day, the second of the three major ceremonies that brought us to Seoul. For this second ceremony, there is to be a small gathering at home, and on the following day a larger celebration at the Hotel Silla.

Haeja, her sisters, and her brothers' wives wear formal green and white hanbok which Mrs. Han has had made for the celebration. All the men of the house wear the dark blue Western-style suits that were made for Mr. Han's hwan-gap, which was celebrated last year. The children wear colorful new clothes.

A photographer circulates through this ever-expanding group of immediate family, recording the event.

There is really no beginning for the hwan-gap, as preparations have gone on for weeks, each day growing more intense with activities. The morning of the celebration, the kitchen is frantic with maids and helpers preparing the meal for fifty or sixty guests that must be served that afternoon. Gradually, over the course of the morning, the Hans' children and grandchildren wander into the house, waiting for everything to begin. Then Mrs. Han's relatives show up, culminating with the arrival of her sisters.

Throughout the morning, various household assistants have made one long, low table by placing smaller ones next to each other, and now two rows of this long table horseshoes the living room; the couches and reading chairs pushed back into corners. Before the meal, various sets of children and husbands and wives must step forward to mother and father, sitting in chairs in the center of the horseshoe of low tables, and present them with a traditional bow: kneel on the floor, extend arms on the floor, touch head to outstretched hands. The movement always gives me a chill, the utter prostration of youth before age. It is perhaps *the* Confucian gesture, not only in this household, but throughout the country.

One by one, starting with the youngest members of the household, the guests go forward, kneel, and bow. Now it is my turn. I can't help smiling. There is no solemnity in me; I am all American, head to toe, and the gesture seems foreign. And because I have a bad back, everyone has been worried that I will bow like a good Confucian and never be able to get up again from that humble position.

"That's all right," Mrs. Han says, slightly embarrassed. "You don't have to bow if you don't want to."

"I want to," I say.

"Let him bow," Mr. Han says, full of mischief in his voice and a gleam in his eyes.

"No, really," says mother.

"I don't mind."

"This is good," Mr. Han laughs.

"Don't bend all the way to the floor," Mrs. Han instructs me. "Make a light bow."

"I'll do a formal bow."

"Leave him alone, Mother."

But I take it slowly, trying to minimize awkwardness. When I get up, I receive a smattering of applause for my effort, and I notice Mrs. Han laughing with her husband now. Her sisters stand off to the side of all this, nodding appreciatively. Americans acting like Koreans are nearly as funny and clownish as Americans trying to speak the native tongue.

"That was good," Hae-Chul says. "You have a lot of guts."

"Guts?" I ask.

"You're always willing to become a part of the family, Michael."

"He is a part of the family," Cousin Yoo says.

"Yes," Hae-Chul agrees. "But he is not afraid to make a fool of himself to be part of the family, which is a sure sign that he really is part of the family now."

After the ceremony, everyone sits in prearranged places at the low tables. In front of me are various celebratory dishes— fish, kim-chee pancakes, Chinese hot chicken, stewed ribs, pressed beef, spinach, bean sprouts, *ko-sari,* bowls of rice, glasses of water, smaller glasses for majuang, sashimi, sweet rice cakes died green with parsley, and a syrupy drink of rice and pine nuts for the end of the meal.

Besides the immediate family, there are a few outsiders who "happened" by, like the old man with a toothache sitting across from me and the gaggle of older women at a separate table in their traditional dresses, looking haughty and disdainful of everything. Part Hollywood gossip columnists, part bit-players in a Molière comedy, these ladies are as much a part of Seoul's landscape as the mountains, always in the background of every event I have attended. Not relatives, not even close friends, not colleagues of Mrs. Han's, they are gossips, matchmakers, and brokers, women crucial to the flow of everyday life—thus they have license to barge in unannounced as they did. Their American equivalent is the sit-com next-door neighbor who always shows up at the most inappropriate time and heads right for the refrigerator.

The ceremony of hwan-gap must account for unexpected guests because this is a kind of open house. Literally anyone who shows up will be seated at the table, and extra places have been set for this contingency. In that sense, everyone has a purpose here today, including the minor players. Yet these ceremonies have a rhythm unlike any theater I am used to; like a Noh drama, the pace is excruciatingly slow, and though nothing seems to happen, the players eventually resolve their dramatic goals over the long course of the ceremony. Already I feel a sense of denouement seizing the room.

Now with the ceremony winding down, Mrs. Han's older sisters excuse themselves early to go home. Some of the men wander off into the garden. Women seem to gather in the dining room. The harpies still pick at the food at their separate table near the windows. One of them calls a maid over.

"Put a little bit of each dish in a bag for me, dear," she says. "My husband is sick and he'll appreciate the food. But leave out the dessert. He's a diabetic and the sugar is no good for him."

"Wrap my leftovers up, too," another says.

"And mine, too," says the third.

The maid gives them a look of contempt, but complies without saying a word.

In keeping with ritual, the party at the Hotel Silla is much larger than the one for immediate family, and once again I am reminded how much protocol informs life on this peninsula. Nothing is done individually, everything must first be discussed by everyone—all parties are considered, compromises are made, and then an action is taken. An American businessman once joked to me about how Korean businessmen play tennis: they stand at the net discussing how they are going to play until their time on the court is up, and they haven't hit the ball once. In the Han household, for weeks on end the sole topic of conversation has been this hwan-gap.

Many of the elements of the sixtieth birthday are typical of a Korean event. There is the pomp of the French restaurant, its floor to ceiling windows looking out over the eastern part of the city from the twenty-third floor. There is the circumstance of the occasion itself: the large gathering of people, all decked out in their finery. The hordes of children strain to behave, then finally abandon all pretense of decorum, running berserk through the restaurant, shouting and jumping around. Photographers snap pictures frantically, while waiters scurry around making final preparations. In many respects the event appears to be no different from a family gathering back in America— say, a confirmation or a bar mitzvah—with the attendant periods of boredom and tension between family members. Yet it is different.

I am only bored if I think about how foreign the surroundings and the people are, and finally, after years of coming here, no one is foreign at all. This is home; this is my family. My obligation as a son-in-law is to participate in the ceremonies, nothing more, nothing less. More than being at an ordinary family event, I respond to the undercurrents in the room, the energy of the children, the tensions that persists even into the bountiful present. Even in prosperity and in the midst of celebration, Seoul breeds anxieties about its future. It comes with the territory. A sadness lingers at the borders of everything. Less than feeling like a bar mitzvah at a Flatbush Avenue catering hall, hwan-gap is like those gala balls found in nineteenth-century Russian novels. Once again, as I felt in Hae-Chul's living room several years ago, Seoul reminds me of Moscow a century earlier, or I should say, it reminds me of that city I think I know from Russian literature of a century ago. The feuds and resolutions of a domestic life are so easily framed by a larger historical context. It is as if, years from this moment, I could say to my grandchildren, "This is what Korea was like in the first throes of democracy."

There are no roaming, drunken uncles, as in my childhood family gatherings; no brawls in the backyard, nor softball games and footraces for overweight men straining against their girths and the possibility of heart failure. The face of this event is placid; but underneath that face, I sense people's ambitions, their hurts, their slights and miscalculations. Korea is a driven place; this is one of its driven families. Excellence is not an ideal but rather an achieveable human goal to them. The desire to do well within the family, at school, and in the work place is an unceasing ambition, quelled only by the decorum of cere-monies such as this, and then only for a few hours. Moments after the hwan-gap ends, people will rush to telephones, telexes, and fax machines to make communication with associ-ates in Hong Kong, Tokyo, Los Angeles, Zurich, London, and New York.

For today's ceremony Byung-Soon has picked out the daughters' dresses, which have a Chinese quality to them; each is a different color, with a floral and jewel design above the left breast; the collar is high, the sleeves long, the cut old-fashioned. Several of the others complain that the dress only looks good on Byung-Soon.

Mrs. Han wears a low key, celadon-colored dress, and only a little makeup. The *eemo* (aunts, but literally mother's sisters), in their hanboks, have painted their faces like 1940s Holly-wood starlets. The brilliant hues of the women contrast with the somber, dark colors of most of the men. I once made the mistake of buying floral-patterned ties in London for several male relatives; when I presented them, the men looked at them as if I had handed them dead fish.

In an attempt to lend color to the occasion, Mrs. Han has bought pastel-colored suits for Hae-Chul, Mr. Lee, and me, and Mr. Lee and Hae-Chul wear blue instead of white shirts, a detail of no consequence anywhere but in Seoul. The paisley

ties are as radical as if I showed up at my grandmother's house
in Brooklyn with a purple Mohawk. In fact, everything in the
restaurant fairly bursts with colors in contrast to a few years
ago when dark, funereal colors would have filled the room.
There are flowers everywhere, cool gray marble floors, green
and beige couches, silvery coffee urns, baby blue fringes on the
china, pale green napkins.

After a milling-around period, the guests are seated accord-
ing to their age and status, the center table being the locus of
everything. From it, the tables radiate in circles around the
room, the youngest relatives seated at tables near the windows.
The waiters bring out the trays laden with non-Korean, hotel
food—shrimp bisque or onion soup with smoked salmon on
the side, followed by salad, then filet mignon. Like the birthday party at the house, the occasion must have a certain feeling
of formal eventlessness to be successful; once we settle into our
meals and small talk, the sense that nothing has happened,
nothing is happening, and nothing will happen, roots itself at
each table—which, I think, is exactly what the Hans intended.
But I have a feeling that someone important to this event is
absent. It isn't until Haeja reminds me of our plans to drive out
to the countryside tomorrow that I realize that the missing
person is Grandma Oh.

As the meal ends, children run around and even under the
tables; grown-ups try to restrain them. Even some of the waiters get into it, but as soon as they capture one child, another
shoots past. In Korea, being a child is still the most joyous
occasion of all, even beyond the pleasure of reaching sixty
years old with a full life behind you.

Across the room, I see Mrs. Han's sisters, haughty and stiff
and well-to-do, sipping their coffee, not speaking, looking

around with great disdain. They must look across the room to see their husbands, for the older generation places women at one table, men at another. I realize that if Grandma Oh were still alive, she probably wouldn't have come to this party: toothless, she couldn't have eaten the meat, and she would have refused to dress up for the occasion. Still, she might have come along for a bowl of soup and the wine, and I imagine her in a corner, smoking her cigarettes, laughing and coughing with the old people she would have been seated with.

Grandma Oh turned sixty right after the Korean War, so there was no chance to celebrate. It was probably a day like any other; she got up, made breakfast, did the laundry, shopped, prepared food for dinner, looked after the children, smoked cigarettes, cursed several people and things, and laughed a lot, both at herself and about her circumstances. The occasion was simply one of being alive for another day, to feed and shelter her young, to complain about the absences of goods, maybe even to offer a Buddhist prayer at night, see a fortune-teller, think about visiting a mansin to perform a kut. High-rise French restaurants did not fit into Grandma Oh's notion of the cosmos, her worldview. Everything in her life happened at sea level, in keeping with the spirit of the mountains that surrounded her life.

"I really miss my grandmother," Haeja says. We seem to be thinking the same thoughts.

Mrs. Han has been making her way around the perimeter of the tables, saying hello and greeting various relatives and friends. When she gets to our table, I tell her how lovely she looks.

"I look like a madame," she says, touching the lacy frills on her pale green dress.

"But it has been a good hwan-gap," says Haeja.

"I'm relieved it's almost over," her mother answers. "Some people turn hwan-gap into a Las Vegas circus, speeches, singing, too much spectacle."

Then she wanders away, shaking hands, giving and getting kisses—forever the politician. Haeja stays to talk with her sister, and I go off for a cigarette with Hae-Chul and some of the other younger men.

The next morning we rise early, eat breakfast quickly, and drive off in several cars into the countryside. After driving for just under two hours, we turn onto a dirt road, and drive for a few more minutes. We have come into the country for the last of the three ceremonies that are the occasions for this visit. The cars pull up in front of an enclosed farmyard. A farmer and his extended family scramble out of the yard to greet the assembly of city visitors. He bows to the Hans, on whose ancestral land this farm sits—his large rural family meeting our equally large urban family.

Grandma Oh died last year, overcome by life and cigarettes and the mortification of outliving her only son. It has taken the Hans months to find the right memorial site for her. Even though she is not technically a member of the Han clan, there was a great deal of concern that the old woman be accorded the best in the afterlife since her own life had been so harsh. At last, a geomancer advised them on this site, and Grandma Oh's remains have been buried, a mound has been built, a stone cut and inscribed. We have come today to honor her. Dear Buddha, I pray, may she rest in peace.

Her burial site lies in a valley surrounded by mountains. The land is flat and good for rice farming. There are paddies everywhere I look, shimmering with silvery water. In the farmyard itself, there is a small vegetable patch, sprouting cabbages, root vegetables, onions, garlic, peppers, corn, and tobacco. The yard teems with clucking chickens, a proud rooster, and a few geese. A huge light brown ox is tethered by a rope looped through a ring in its nose and tied to a spike in the ground. The earth breeds a muddy yellow color and the odor of decay. When the city kids attempt to pet the ox's musky hide, the farmer shouts for them to stay away. The animal has work to do and should not be disturbed; it is ornery and dangerous around strangers.

This country setting reminds me that Korea has only been an industrial nation for a few decades and that its roots, going back centuries, are agricultural and rural, just like Grandma Oh. I was told on the drive out that the site where she is buried was deemed auspicious, because this community south of Seoul had endured relatively few invasions and battles; that it had few bad tempered ghosts and demons. The roll of the hillside behind the farmland was thought to capture the spirit of who Grandma Oh was.

"Pally, pally," shouts the farmer, "Quickly, quickly." He shoos the children to the other side of the farmyard where his own kids stare and giggle, first at the well-dressed boys and girls from the big city, then at the man with the gigantic nose—me.

But then it begins to pour and everyone takes refuge under huge black umbrellas for the walk into the woodline, the ground sodden and muddy, and the humidity, heat, and rain drawing off more odors from the land.

Soon the offal smells give way to rich loamy ones in the center of the paddy. We walk in single file, carefully navigating the high ground so as not to fall into the murky paddy water. Since I am the slackman, covering the rear as it were, I have the best angle to appreciate the long line of umbrellas and women in pretty dresses and bright city shoes that are getting ruined by the muddy ground. It is like a scene in a movie, a strange combination of the funereal and the festive—children laughing and singing, adults joking with one another. The sound of the rain on the umbrellas creates a pleasant music to this living cinema.

After about ten minutes, I am so far in the rear that I no longer see the farmer leading the way, nor the children dancing along behind him. A black snake slithers off in the murk of the paddy; jackdaws screech in the pine tops. In spite of the laughter and chatter up ahead, a sad song works through my head.

My clearest image of Grandma Oh is from the last time we saw her alive. By then she had become so feeble and withered that staying alive was nothing but an indignity to her. She was full of aches and pains, and nothing seemed to work any-more—not her limbs, her mouth, her eyes, or even her brain. Her breathing was labored and her mind wandered aimlessly. She had lung cancer, emphysema, arthritis and rheumatism; her eyes glassed over with cataracts. Years of walking up and down the hilly roads of Taegu and Seoul had made her heart nearly indestructible, but everything else about her had eroded from years of use. Her bones were brittle; her gums swelled and bled; knots of her hair fell out; her tiny fingers gnarled into fists which took great effort to uncurl.

The rain lets up momentarily and the gaps in the procession close up. The women joke about their ruined shoes; children chatter about snakes in the paddy or owls in the pines. Some of the men smoke, staring off at the beautiful panorama of mountains.

The trail widens, and people walk two and three abreast, commenting on the serenity and grandeur of Grandma Oh's gravesite. Mr. Han's geomancers have chosen well. As is the custom, Grandma Oh's body is not interred beneath the ground, but rather is covered by an elevated earthen mound, in front of which is positioned a strikingly simple rectangular, granite monument inscribed: "Lady Kim Lon"—that is Grandma's maiden name—"of Taegu Rests Here."

A Buddhist by nature, a folk worshiper by temperament, a good woman of the Confucian orders, a believer in fortune-tellers and geomancers, Grandma is now part of the Korean earth. She is a memory, or in terms of the belief systems of the Korean world, she is now our esteemed ancestor. As such, she is as good as a god, maybe even better, because she is a spirit with whom we have an inside track. Free of her aches, her voice now is part of this landscape.

I sit on a granite bench in front of the gravesite and watch the women and children and men lay wreathes and flowers on the grave, some of them offering up either Buddhist prayers or mysterious animist chants, the mansin whispers that intrigued Grandma Oh, gave her comfort and focus.

The sky clears momentarily and a rainbow appears behind the gravesite, not arcing upward into the heavens, but vertical and seeming to emanate from the site as though it was Grandma herself, wearing, as she never did in her adult life, a rainbow-colored long flowing hanbok. I take out my in-stamatic camera and capture it. I am tempted to ask Haeja and the others whether they too saw the rainbow, but the family is in a deeply Korean mode—my English would be an intrusion. I'll have to wait until the film is developed to know for certain.

Everyone makes two deep, formal bows to the stone, first Mr. Han, then the other men, then the women and children. Rice wine is poured over the grave and more formal bows are made—one may bow as often as one likes, so long as it is not an odd number of times, which is unlucky. At the altar in front of the stone, red food (hot pepper sauce) is placed toward the east, white (pickled turnips) toward the west. Several of the men leave cigarettes, and one of the girls leaves an ashtray for Grandma Oh.

Soon another barrage of rain clouds works overhead, and the next burst of monsoon waters crash down. We open the black umbrellas and slowly drift off, carefully working our way down the hillside.

Somehow the Hans' driver has brought the car to the base of the hill. Mrs. Han tries to insist that I ride with her husband back to the farmyard, but I tell her that the rain does not bother me, and I am looking forward to walking back along the berm, breathing its loamy perfume and watching the raindrops scatter on the surface of the silvery water, and the magpies flit about in the tall pines. I'm never able to spend enough time in the country, and I can't help but feel that this landscape literally is Grandma Oh now; I really have a sense of her as I walk back to the farmyard, down the hill and through the paddy. If Seoul is Korea's pulse, the countryside remains its backbone.

I try to use up my remaining film because I want to get it developed immediately back in the city. Standing far enough away from the ox to keep the farmer happy, I snap photographs of the children, of the less camera-shy adults, and the farmer and his children, who can't help covering their faces with their hands and giggling; they squirm and move and try to duck behind each other to get away from the camera.

When the time comes to leave, it's hard for me to tear myself away. In a world like this one, a woman like Grandma Oh neither dies nor fades away. Her beliefs allow her to come back into the world lucky like a rabbit, turtle, or deer. At worst, she might become a carp, waiting a thousand years to become a dragon.

> As a carp ascends to heaven,
> The moon rises through the corn husks
> And water in the rice field
> Turns to silver; the poplars shimmer
> In the moonlight like quilled pens
> And the tawny owl hoos of summer.
> The carp ascends to heaven, breaking
> Through the smoky surface of night water,
> Bursting upward like a scaled jet—
> By morning it becomes a dragon.

ABOUT THE AUTHOR

MICHAEL STEPHENS is a novelist, playwright, poet, and journalist. His previous work includes two novels, *Season at Coole* and *Shipping Out*, the one-act "Our Father" and other plays, and collections of short fiction, poetry, and essays. He teaches in the Creative Writing Program at Princeton University and lives in New York City.